Architect for Art Max Gordon

Marquand Books, Seattle

Architect for Art Max Gordon

Max Gordon
David Gordon
Nicholas Serota
Kenneth Frampton
Doris Lockhart Saatchi
Charles Saatchi
Jackie Brody
David Juda
Keith and Kathy Sachs
Lewis and Susan Manilow
Emily Fisher Landau
Jonathan Marvel

Contents

Preface

David Gordon

Max Gordon was an important figure in the small contemporary art world of the 1960s and 1970s as a collector, friend, and encourager of younger artists and their fledgling gallerists. Once he set up his own architectural practice in 1981, he became a significant figure for the rest of the decade as a pioneer in the design of unobtrusive spaces in which contemporary art could be shown to best advantage and in which lovers of art could live enjoyably with their collections. His palpable love for contemporary art and his combination of shyness, sociability, and humor made him a figure both admired and loved.

Max died prematurely at the age of fifty-nine in 1990 from an AIDS-related illness, just before contemporary art began its explosive growth. Why a book now, two decades later?

First, after the excesses of all kinds, including in architecture, of the recent past, it is time for a return to an architecture infused with a spirit of minimalism, simplicity, and economy. That spirit, summed up in the title of Kenneth Frampton's essay in this book, "Almost Nothing," has perhaps been kept alive mostly in contemporary art galleries. Max can claim some credit: his Soho galleries of the 1980s have been a powerful influence on those that followed in Chelsea in subsequent years. This influence deserves to be acknowledged. Richard Gluckman, one of the current architects of choice for contemporary art spaces, was Max's New York associate for five years; Andrew Ong, another fine gallery architect, was an associate, too. In art museums, the recent boom has produced few buildings that are both distinguished and good for showing art. Tate Modern, a conversion of an old building, is one exception. In his essay, Nicholas Serota, the director of the Tate, cites Max's influence on the project and attributes to Max the creation of the Turner Prize.

Second, a book was mooted after his death, but those involved were too preoccupied to see it through to completion. In my case, I went from being the C.E.O. of *The Economist* magazine to running a television news station before becoming secretary of the Royal Academy of Arts and then director of the Milwaukee Art Museum. The switch into the arts was a result of the assumption that I shared some of Max's art genes. When Norman Rosenthal, its exhibitions secretary, tapped me to come to the Royal Academy, he said it needed a person with my business experience to run things and, besides, the clincher: "You are Max's brother." My dozen years as a museum director were demanding, yet extremely rewarding, but it is only since breaking the shackles of employment that I have had the time and energy to return to this project. This book is my way of saying thanks to Max.

Compiling this book has also made me realize, humbly, that none of us ever truly knew Max, not even me, his own brother. A book meant to present a selection of his architectural contributions also quickly became a book about the way Max moved in the world, in part because his personal life and friendships were critical to the commissions he would receive. It is also a way for me to get to know him better.

This is a story about a man who came of age when homosexuality was illegal and, therefore, whose life became necessarily fragmented and private, even for someone with adoring friends. It is with a certain wistfulness that his friends imagine what Max might have done for architecture and, therefore, for art had he lived. Put another way, what if Max had been alive at a time when he could have been fully known and lived a long life? As Agnes Gund, president emerita of the Museum of Modern Art expressed to me: "I remember feeling so much that he would have built some very important buildings—a masterpiece of design. He had such promise to do more and more."

Those involved in the production of this book hope that it will appeal to a wide audience: to those who make art and think about how it should be displayed; to those who enjoy looking at art and wonder why contemporary art looks right in some galleries, homes, and museums and not in others; and to artists, collectors, curators, architects, designers, and everyone with a strong visual sense—those who both look and see. It is a book about an architect, but it is not burdened with technical information. Max's characteristic way of working was to look, talk to the client, sketch out his ideas, talk to the client again, and then, once the concept was secure, assign an associate architect to make working drawings and supervise construction. So this book is full of sketches and photographs.

The arrangement of the book is straightforward. It begins with the text of a talk that Max was due to deliver in 1990 that sets out clearly and lucidly his ideas about museums of contemporary art. Three essays follow, and seven major projects are introduced by the clients—except in the case of Max's own apartment—concluding with a summary of Max's architectural characteristics and a chronology and list of works enlivened by quotations from those involved in those projects. Transcripts of interviews conducted in the preparation of the book will be archived. The Avery Architectural and Fine Arts Library, Columbia University, New York, is the repository of his architectural archive and the Tate Archive, London, of his art and personal archive. I am grateful to Janet Parks, curator of prints and drawings at the Avery, and to Adrian Glew, Tate archivist, for their enthusiasm and professionalism.

Most of the many people to whom I spoke in preparing this book were delighted to know that it was forthcoming, and I hope that their expectations are met. I would like to thank in particular those who talked about, and in some cases wrote about and secured photography of, the seven featured projects: Doris Lockhart Saatchi, Charles Saatchi, Jackie Brody, David Juda, Keith and Kathy Sachs, Lewis and Susan Manilow, Emily Fisher Landau, Bill Katz, and Nicholas Arbatsky. Doris Lockhart Saatchi has kindly given permission for a chapter adapted from her forthcoming memoirs to be used as the main text on 98a Boundary Road and permission to reproduce her photographs of the gallery. While 98a Boundary Road is its proper name, the space has been referred to as the Saatchi Collection or the Saatchi Gallery, and reference is made to it in these various ways by others in the book. Doris is also the author of a 1976 *World of Interiors* article on 120 Mount Street, and thanks are due to the publisher Condé Nast for permission to reproduce it here. Doris also curated an exhibition on Max at the Architecture Foundation in 1992 with the apposite title *No Trim.* It is not too late to again thank the then-director of the foundation, Richard Burdett, for that important show.

I would also like to thank the many others who shared memories and insights into Max. In alphabetical order these were David Acheson, Pierre Apraxine, Monique Barbier-Mueller, Jennifer Bartlett, Robert Bell, Natalie de Blois, Stephen Buckley, Richard Burdett, Catherine Cahill and Bill Bernhard, R. G. Chapman, Carol Coffin, Peter Collymore, Paula Cooper and Jack Macrae, Dagny Corcoran, Jim Corcoran, Douglas Cramer, Sylvia de Cuevas, Jack Dunbar, Jane Durham, Kit Evans, Frederick Fisher, Kaj Forsblom, Adrian Gale, Carmen Gimenez, Richard Gluckman, Robert Gober, Nadia Goedhuis, Richard Goldsbrough, Charles Gordon, Sidney Gordon, Jacqueline Green, John Guest, Agnes Gund, Jan Hashey, Gill Hedley, Alanna Heiss, Howard Hodgkin, Bob Holman, Robert and Randi Israel, Minja Ivanovic, Barbara Jakobson, Eva Jiricna, Dakis Joannou, Jasper Johns, Allen Jones, John Kaldor, Alex Katz, Vivien Katz, Enid Kirchberger, Mark Lancaster, John "Jack" Lane, Julian Lethbridge, Susan Lorence and Robert Monk, Lawrence Luhring, Steve Martin, Helen McEachrane, Kynaston McShine, Adelaide de Menil, Keith Milow, Richard Morphet, Rosemary Morse, Victoria Newhouse, Andrew Ong, Ellen Phelan and Joel Shapiro, Jennifer Radford, Roger Radford, Amia Raphael, Peter Schlesinger, Penelope Seidler, Richard Serra, Sylvia Simon, Betsy Smith, Richard Smith, Joseph Sonnabend, Yolanda Sonnabend, Jill Spalding, Joanne Stern, Rick Stich, Scott Teas, Jeanne Thayer, Alan Turner, John Vinci and Philip Hamp, Leslie Waddington, Felicity Waley-Cohen, Benjamin Weese, Ealan Wingate, Jennifer Winkworth, Jackie Winsor, Laura-Lee Woods, Nigel Woolner, and Joe Zucker.

Those most closely concerned with the making of this book deserve special thanks. Jonathan Marvel, of Rogers Marvel Architects—who went to meet Max in the mid-1980s because he was so keen on his work—in general for his architectural insights, and in particular for his summary of Max's architectural characteristics; also for his superb drawings of some of Max's plans, his many creative suggestions, as well as the use of his firm's office, and for finding Elizabeth Dietz. Liz was the initial research assistant, and she produced a fine dummy. Following Max's example, I went in search of young talent and was fortunate to find it in the hard-working and cool-headed project editor, Holiy LaDue—thanks to our mutual friend Julia Rydholm for recommending her former Phaidon colleague—and the designer Matthew Egan, who is clearly a Maxist. Maggi Gordon took time off from her fourteenth quilt book to proofread the text. We self-published to the camera-ready stage but were helped all the way to the printers by Ed Marquand, Adrian Lucia, Becky Schomer, Keryn Means, and Sara Billups of Marquand Books. We are grateful to D.A.P./Distributed Art Publishers, in particular Elisa Leshowitz, for distributing the book in the United States and to Art Data for distributing it in the United Kingdom. This book has been published first in the U.S., but economics did not allow a separate edition for the U.K. The spelling, usage, and punctuation, therefore, are American English. What the British call the ground floor, for example, is here the first floor.

This is a picture book, and Max was fortunate that magazines and his clients had commissioned excellent photography of his projects. I would like to thank the photographers who have honored and preserved Max's architecture over the years.

Finally, heartfelt thanks to Nicholas Serota, who took time out of an incredibly busy life to write a fine and carefully researched essay, and to Kenneth Frampton for elaborating on the piece he wrote for the catalogue for the 1992 *No Trim* exhibition.

New Museum Architecture and Contemporary Art

Max Gordon

Museums have now taken on an urban function. Due to the iniquities of town planning and the increasing irritation and danger caused by traffic, it has become difficult to use cities in a functional way and there are fewer public places to meet. So museums have become places to walk about in, to see things and people. They have increasingly taken on the role of spaces for what are now called "leisure activities." This has led to museums having to be more entertaining. People who run museums feel that they must have restaurants and bookshops and gift shops and theaters, as well as the necessary conservation and storage facilities. They must have several exhibitions on at the same time and continual blockbuster shows to maintain interest. Museums have to raise money and they therefore host benefit galas and have become a center of social activities.

This has led to the erection of many museums which the prominent people of cities feel gives their city a metropolitan prestige. Because of the social standing of museums and the people involved, the architecture of these museums becomes a very significant factor and most of the best architects today have been involved in the creation of these new monuments.

Architects have seized the opportunity to create lavish institutions to cope with all the uses that museums now need, and one after the other demonstrates an overwhelming architectural expression. But, what has happened to the art? I find that most architects are ignorant of, and uninterested in art. In fact, they are actively hostile to it. I suspect that architects like to control the spaces they are designing and are therefore suspicious of art that is surprising and unexpected. They feel that art must be subservient to the building. Therefore the art is drowned by the architectural treatment. It is most unusual for architects to accept that the art is the most important element of the museum and therefore be able to design quiet rooms that allow the art to breathe.

A large part of the fault lies with the brief with which architects are presented, which results from the uncertainty of what the museum is supposed to be doing. Is it supposed to be carefully building up a collection and having shows which reveal the quality of its artworks? Or is it supposed to put on blockbuster shows, to attract the large mass of the public and flourish its enormous attendance figures, caring less for quality or ease of viewing.

I prefer the former solution and feel that rather than spend millions on an impressive monument it is far better to have harmonious rooms. This is particularly so for the art of the 1960s and 1970s when spatial considerations were of paramount importance to the artists. It is better to devote money to the works of key artists in depth, whatever the size of the works, rather than get indifferent, smaller, and more manageable works of more artists in order to fill gaps in art-historical terms. Purchased works should be carefully studied and arranged to be able to realize fully the artists' intentions, and the prime purpose of the building is to respect this consideration. A museum should be a place of enlightenment and study and not a cultural supermarket.

My central point is that everything possible must be done to allow pictures to breathe and be enjoyed without distraction.

Edited extract from a text by Max Gordon for a conference held at the Des Moines Art Center, Iowa, on April 28–29, 1990. Due to Gordon's illness the paper was read in his absence.

Max Gordon, 1985

Gordon in a friend's Morgan
car, c. 1970s

My Brother Max

David Gordon

I found a rare diary entry made when my brother Max was fourteen and I was four: "Another boring day. David, a perfect pest." The entry reveals, besides my pestiness, several Max characteristics: an ability to communicate concisely and directly, and a dislike of inactivity. Its rarity is symptomatic of a reluctance to journalizing or introspection. Nonetheless, he kept every scrap of paper that ever passed through his hands, including an occasional bus ticket and all his old school exercise books, in bulging manila folders, and piles of shirts recorded an ever-increasing neck size in his meticulous closet.

The incomplete, abbreviated Max depicted in this essay is constructed not only from my memories and from talking to friends and family, but also from the archive he left behind. Biographical, but not a biography, this essay concentrates on the formative influences that made him important in the world of contemporary art and architecture in the 1980s.

The Gordon Family

Our parents passed on genes for energy, humor, and art to Max. Sholom Gordon and Tania Kovner married in their hometown of Vilnius, Lithuania, in 1921 and had two children, Amy and Charles. In 1929 they immigrated to Cape Town, South Africa, where they had two more children, Max and Sidney. They found South Africa provincial and, showing great enterprise, moved a second time, just before World War II, to England, where I was born.

Sholom, a warm, generous, and big-hearted man, was a businessman with a flair for sales and a tremendous sense of humor. Tania, or, as our father called her, "The Duchess of Hampstead," also had a larger-than-life personality, vivacious and exuberant, extolling life, art, and creation. They were both gregarious. She took up painting in her fifties, wielding a palette knife to depict flowers in thick oils, becoming a talented and original self-taught artist.

Max was shy, quiet, and reserved, with a very English suspicion of public displays of emotion or discussion of his feelings. As I mention in the Preface, being homosexual in a country where homosexuality was not legalized until he was thirty-six must have added to a quest for privacy. However, Max himself eventually became outgoing like his parents. He could be quite a performer, entertaining audiences, particularly of well-bred ladies, with his wit and enthusiasm. He loved art and those who made it, but found it difficult himself to love a partner.

Education

Max endured rather than enjoyed school. He and Sidney were sent to Portsmouth Grammar School because there they could board with a dozen other Jewish boys in a house run by a rabbi. Max loathed it, and thereafter was never interested in anything Jewish other than the jokes and the food. He cooked excellent latkes. If obliged to go to synagogue he secreted a copy of *The Spectator* magazine into the prayer book.

Max was a creative young person, drawing, writing, and reading widely, and even building himself a room in the garden at home where he lived. He almost studied English at university until Amy reminded him of his first love: when he was twelve, he declared one day that he would become an architect when he grew up.

He went to Christ's College, Cambridge, and came into his own academically and socially. Architecture was taught in a traditional way. Students had to learn lettering and cycle into the countryside to draw churches. This stood him in good stead: he learned to draw freehand quickly and clearly. His contemporaries remember Max as better informed about international developments in architecture than other students or the faculty and as a very social animal while being shy and reserved and a bit uptight. He chortled a lot and had the tendency to burst into hysterical laughter before finishing a joke. His submission to the *Architects' Journal* for a "Long-weekend House" was a drawing of a long house with a weak end. For one of his projects at Cambridge he submitted an elaborate "Booth for a Wealthy Fortune Teller." Max's education as an architect was protracted and thorough. The Architectural Association in London, one of the best architectural schools in England, was stimulating and demanding, and after graduation from Cambridge he did three years of professional training there. While at the AA from 1952 to 1955, he lived at the family home in Hampstead, where his room was an island of modernity, inspired by the 1951 Festival of Britain. He had a black Rover car with all the chrome painted matte black. *No Trim*, the title suggested by his artist friend Stephen Buckley for the memorial exhibition held at the Architecture Foundation in The Economist Building in 1992, captured his emerging style.

Significantly, a huge black-and-white reproduction of "The Ideal City" by Piero della Francesca, painted by a friend, hung in his room. It epitomized his quest for the ideal, for perfect proportions, for a sense of perspective in both meanings of the term. Max's version had noblemen walking in a city that in the original is completely bereft of humans. Architecture for him was meant to enhance the experience of living.

Postwar England in the mid-1950s was depleted of resources and energy, while America was alluring and promising. Max's admiration for American can-do boldness and for doing things "properly" remained undimmed all his life. In 1955 he arrived for a one-year Master's course at the Harvard Graduate School of Design, where the dean, Josep Lluís Sert, took a broad view of architecture, stressing the importance of aesthetics, design, and the wider political world. Sert was an ardent modernist, a disciple of Le Corbusier, whose chapel at Ronchamp and the Unité d'Habitation in Marseille Max had visited in 1954. From Le Corbusier's teachings Max learned space, volume, and a refusal to be tentative.

Career

But these concepts were moderated by admiration for the rectilinear elegance of Mies van der Rohe, so it was natural for him to gravitate after graduation to the New York office of Skidmore, Owings & Merrill, designers of Miesian office buildings on an industrial scale under the disciplining leadership of Gordon Bunshaft, an avid art collector. The office was busy, and architects were given a lot of leeway, but they had to perform. Max worked on the midtown executive suite and boardroom of the Chase Manhattan Bank at 410 Park Avenue, as well as the Banque Lambert in Brussels. The clients for both projects, David Rockefeller and Léon Lambert, were art collectors who believed in having art in offices, undoubtedly another important influence on him. The SOM office was productive but not pleasant, and after six years he left to return to Britain.

Max's next two positions were in London. In 1962 he became a partner at Chapman, Taylor and Partners, a firm set up in 1958 by Cambridge friends. While there, Max led the design of New Scotland Yard. He was also the architect of a plastics factory at Cramlington. The engineering was faulty with the result that CTP had to make a hefty restitution payment, which was used as an opportunity to sever relations between Max and the other partners. A colleague wrote in sadness that he had brought balance to a firm that "leans too heavily in the direction of Mammon."

Our brother Charles, then making a name for himself in London's financial world, was involved in a large scheme for the Brighton Marina, and in 1970 he helped Max obtain a partnership at Louis de Soissons, the firm carrying out the design. Charles had been an important influence on Max's life. Max went to Charles's college at Cambridge, and Charles had reintroduced him to John Taylor and Bob Chapman. Married to the prima ballerina Nadia Nerina, Charles at times also helped Max financially and introduced him into their

Top: Geodesic dome built by Gordon while he was studying at the AA

Bottom: Le Corbusier's Chapel of Notre Dame du Haut, Ronchamp, France

Opposite: Gordon's bedroom in Hampstead

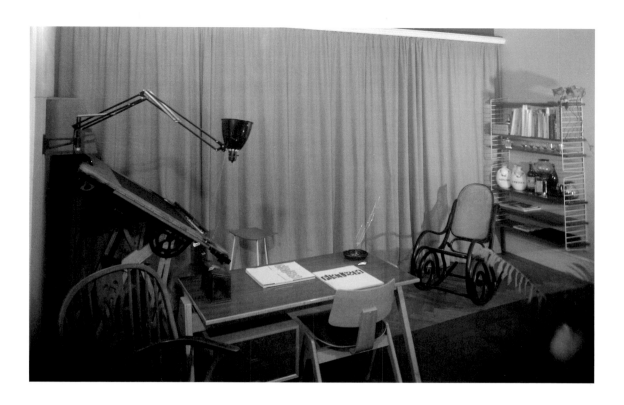

glamorous social world. But his helpfulness may have had a lead lining: only when he was fifty did Max, who had been unhappy as a partner of commercial practices, set up his own independent firm.

Max Gordon Associates

Max Gordon Associates began to design spaces for art and flourished. Max quickly devised a method of working that was as elegant and spare as his designs. He worked with the client to create the design concept and then outsourced the detailed drawings and construction supervision to another architect. In general, Max and the associate architect would contract with the clients separately for fees of around five and fifteen percent respectively. In London his associate was Richard Goldsbrough. In New York he worked mostly with Richard Gluckman, who went on to be a highly successful architect specializing in galleries and museums. Max worked from home or on-site without assistants or secretaries, Pentel in hand, sketching alternatives on tracing paper in a live seminar with the clients. His records consist of handdrawn sketches and fading hand-written faxes. Contracts were short or nonexistent, allowing him to be both mobile and very productive.

Max's clients came from networks of friends and acquaintances built up over decades looking for and at contemporary art. He knew the small number of London dealers in contemporary art, such as Anthony d'Offay, for whom he did a gallery on Dering Street; Annely Juda, for whom he later did the space upstairs; and Nigel Greenwood, through whom he met Gilbert and George. There were also few collectors in London then. His friendship with Charles and Doris Saatchi led to the 1983 commission for the Saatchi Gallery on Boundary Road, which in turn led to his becoming the go-to architect for art spaces after it opened two years later.

While at SOM in the 1950s, he was a member of the Junior Council of the Museum of Modern Art, and in 1972 was invited to join the International Council. He also became the only non-American on the museum's trustee committee on architecture and design. The council, a prestigious group of museum supporters and collectors of contemporary art from around the world, mostly but not exclusively wealthy, travel as a group twice a year to see art. Its members became an important part of his social life, and Max became a great favorite of a cohort of elegant, witty, and well-informed ladies.

Max's friendships led to commissions and vice versa. Paula Cooper was his great friend downtown, and she discussed each iteration of her Wooster Street gallery with him. The apartment above the gallery, and subsequently a guest suite in her and her husband's house on West 21st Street that he also remodeled, provided homes for his extended stays in New York. He was a good friend of Joel Shapiro and Ellen Phelan, buying a miniature ladder from Joel's first show at the Clocktower Gallery in 1973 and designing their apartment a dozen years later. In 1972 he acquired from Paula a major piece by Jennifer Bartlett, "Surface Substitution on 36 Plates," now in the Tate's collection. For Jennifer he did an apartment in Paris and remodeled her New York apartment. Jennifer in turn remodeled Max into the character Harry Warner in her book, *The History of the Universe*. He did apartments for Richard Serra and Elizabeth Murray. Brooke Alexander and Ealan Wingate were among the gallerists who became clients and remained friends. He knew most of the curators and museum directors in the contemporary art field.

The opportunities grew as the museum building boom got under way. In 1987 he designed a Beverly Hills house for actor Steve Martin, and his wife, the actress Victoria Tennant, but it was not realized because they moved to New York instead. Max left a sketch for the interior spaces of the Paul J. Schupf wing at the Museum of Art, Colby College, Maine, that houses a gift of works from Alex Katz, another friend. The concept for the interiors and the roof were retained in the final, posthumously completed work.

His international reputation led to a residence and gallery in Greece for the collector Dakis Joannou but were never built, the Gallery Kaj Forsblom in Helsinki, Finland, discussions with Bruno Bischofberger in Zurich, Switzerland, and an unbuilt studio for Anselm Kiefer in Germany. His name was in circulation just as the art museum building boom of the past two decades got going: he was on the short list for the San Francisco Museum of Contemporary Art in 1988 and for the Museum zeitgenössische Kunst (Museum for Contemporary Art) in Stuttgart, Germany, in 1990.

Illness

Max's premature death at the age of fifty-nine came about from a series of sexually transmitted illnesses. He caught severe non-A, non-B hepatitis, now called hepatitis-C, in 1983, which later turned into cirrhosis of the liver. He knew the dangers and causes of the AIDS epidemic of the early 1980s. His New York doctor, Joseph Sonnabend, a brother of one of his oldest friends, theater designer Yolanda Sonnabend, was a pioneer researcher of the transmission mechanism among gay men. Tested regularly by Sonnabend for HIV, he tested positive in 1988. The interaction between cirrhosis, the HIV virus, and the medicines he was taking for both, started giving him nosebleeds that would not stop. In April 1990 he was rushed to the hospital in a coma and after massive blood transfusions rallied. The doctor asked Max if he had any questions. "Yes," said Max, "what's my estimated shelf life?" He died four months later.

It is difficult to explain why someone so controlled, organized, successful, and popular, would take such risks, particularly as he had at least two long-term affairs of the heart. One was with a teacher in New York, Gerry Franchina, whose letters show him trying to get Max to admit his love and commit and who accused him of using the return to London in 1962 as an excuse to break up. Another relationship was with Howard Hodgkin for two or three years in the early 1980s, that inspired three of Howard's paintings, one of which is owned by Max's clients Keith and Kathy Sachs (page 133).

People were his elixir. His greetings to friends were effusive, especially to his many women friends. I was at his hospital bedside when he was very sick in New York. The phone would ring, and I would ask a near-comatose Max if he wanted to speak to, say, Victoria Tennant. He instantly perked up and seized the phone. "Victoria! My darling, how are you? What's going on?"

Max was passionate about art. His eye was not just good, it was impeccable, and it glinted. His judgment about art, architecture, and design—his holy trinity—was sure-fire, as visitors to his Mount Street apartment

appreciated. His vocabulary was rich with terms of judgement: "coherent," "simple," "appropriate," and "well-organized" were words of approval. "Hideous," "monstrous," "outrageous," and "unspeakable" were his favorite epithets of condemnation. In addition, Max had a range of sounds. There was a negative "humph," or a mediating "hmmmm," or an "I see," which could mean either that he did or that he did not, depending on the intonation.

An unpatronizing patron of artists, he cherished his friends, entertained them graciously, and made them laugh with his one-liners. When Jennifer Bartlett married Mattieu Carrière, she was "in mid-carriere." "Help, I'm Salle-vating." Norman Rosenthal became "Roman Nosenthal."

When he was twenty-one, he jotted down a few thoughts on Christ's College letterhead:

I write this as I obtain my majority, here in the tranquility of a Cambridge street with the sweet air passing through and the transcendental music. Twenty-one. What do I feel? Mature? A full man? Able to face the world? I have always felt that the world is a jungle and that one must be strong to survive and am I? Surely. I feel I could tackle it all. Fresh goals, limitless horizons, unhampered in heart and yet one must have unrecognized as yet restrictions. Will I keep the enthusiasm I have always had? The clear, open, vibrant life and the joy of creation? How many others feel it?

Max kept the enthusiasm and the joy of creation, but was overpowered by the jungle within.

Two examples of the many drawings Gordon created

Gallery designed by Gordon
for the Museo Reina Sofía,
with Richard Serra's "Equal-
Parallel; Guernica Bengasi,"
1986

The Artists' Friend

Nicholas Serota

Max Gordon was a genuine cosmopolitan, equally at home in London, New York, or in the home of a sophisticated collector in Chicago. Though he studied architecture at some of the world's best institutions, his essential formation as an architect occurred during the six years he spent in New York working with the most accomplished of the postwar generation of modernist architects, Skidmore, Owings & Merrill. In London Gordon was distinctive. He moved easily between the social worlds of Chelsea, Kensington, and Mayfair, inhabited by collectors, interior designers, pop celebrities, and minor royalty, and the studios of emerging artists in Butler's Wharf or Covent Garden. He was a close friend of artists and at parties in his refined apartment in Belgrave Square and later on Mount Street, he would gather his worlds together in bright conversation with the latest gossip and news from New York and the West Coast. Max Gordon had style.

Gordon was something of a rarity, an architect with a passion for art who was in turn loved and admired by artists. Many architects associate with artists, and some succeed in designing spaces in which the art rather than the architecture is paramount. However, very few architects are regarded as friends and equals by artists, let alone accomplish this feat on both sides of the Atlantic. Garrulous but shy, given to one-liners but never glib, Max Gordon was a central figure in the London and New York art worlds for more than twenty years, from the late sixties until his early death at the age of fifty-nine in 1990.

Both as a host and a guest, he was generous, appearing at the end of a long day when everyone else was tired in one of his freshly laundered shirts with a whole string of newly minted one-liners. He brought insight and gossip in equal measure, passed on in pithy, sharp but never very unkind summaries of character and behavior. For many years his practice as an architect, working in the modernist tradition learned from his close association with Gordon Bunshaft at SOM, was little known to his artist friends. However, in his early fifties he established Max Gordon Associates, and after a difficult first year or two, persuaded the collectors Charles and Doris Saatchi to transform a former paint warehouse in north London into one of the most satisfying spaces anywhere for looking at art. The success of the project at 98a Boundary Road brought commissions from private collectors, galleries, and small public museums across Europe and America, establishing an aesthetic in museum architecture that still has influence a quarter of a century later.

Early Connections

Gordon's success could not have been predicted. After he returned to England in the sixties, he was regarded by his English associates largely as a good friend and a giver of excellent parties. He was tightly connected to a generation of modernist, abstract artists and performers working in the wake of Jasper Johns and Robert Rauschenberg in art and John Cage and Merce Cunningham in music and dance. In New York, Soho was his milieu, with artists and dealers—especially Paula Cooper—his closest friends. In Manhattan he was regarded as a much more serious player, an Englishman with a rare passion for contemporary visual arts who was an active member of the International Council of the Museum of Modern Art, the group of international collectors who give support to the Museum's programs abroad. In the 1970s he became a springboard into New York for a generation of British artists, including Michael Craig-Martin, Keith Milow, Stephen Buckley, and Tim Head, and provided a welcome in London for visiting artists such as Brice Marden, Richard Serra, and Jennifer Bartlett.

Gordon was never an establishment figure in England. In spite of his long association with the Museum of Modern Art, he never felt comfortable as a committee man and did not join boards in London until his early fifties. Instead, he preferred to give support to artists in a more personal way. Though never wealthy, he would acquire work from friends, often at a critical stage in their careers. In the 1970s he assembled one of the most adventurous collections of contemporary British and American art in London, including important pieces by Johns, Marden, Bartlett, Buckley, Craig-Martin, Lee Bontecou, Sol LeWitt, Barry Flanagan, Joel Shapiro, and Elizabeth Murray, later adding work by artists emerging in the 1980s such as Robert Gober, Lisa Milroy, Mark Wallinger, and Carroll Dunham.

The King's Square Show and the Whitechapel Gallery

In 1973 his frustration with the lack of ambition in London public art institutions, coupled with friendships established in New York, generated a characteristically ambitious project for a show of new American art to be mounted in a group of vacant warehouse spaces off King's Road in Chelsea. The practice where he worked, Louis de Soissons, had been commissioned to develop a mixed-use scheme on the one-and-a-half-acre site. In the spring of 1973, Gordon became the chair of the committee organizing the *King's Square Show*. The plan was for an exhibition in the buildings before they were demolished. Selected by Barbara Rose, the distinguished American critic, the exhibition was intended to show what the prospectus termed "post-object art," promising "it will contain three elements, environments, media and performance."[1] The show was scheduled for July 4 to August 8, 1973, and the plan was to commission environments, present a continuous showing of film and videotapes, and stage a ten-day festival of performance, music, dance, and theater.

Among the artists invited were Keith Sonnier, Bruce Nauman, Serra, LeWitt, John Chamberlain, Donald Judd, Robert Irwin, Michael Snow, Philip Glass, Mabou Mines, Joan Jonas, Trisha Brown, and Robert Whitman. The film and video program included Peter Campus, Robert Morris, Yvonne Rainer, and Robert Smithson. The range of artists and the character of the venue were unprecedented in London, and probably only Max Gordon could have orchestrated such a venture at that time. Cocktail parties to raise funds were held in New York and London, but the plans came to nothing, probably because sufficient funding could not be secured. However, the project was widely discussed in the London art world and it gave additional weight to the discussion of the minimal and emerging post-minimal work that was being shown at a small number of London galleries such as Nigel Greenwood, Situation, and Lisson.

In the early 1980s, after Gordon left Louis de Soissons and established his own practice, he began to engage with the non-commercial sector of the London art world and became an influential trustee of the Whitechapel Gallery. The gallery, having embarked on a program of expansion and modernization, looked to Gordon for advice on design. As a trustee, he could not compete for the position of architect, and to his sometimes obvious frustration, his role was limited to guidance and occasional frank criticism. John Miller and Alan Colquhoun had been selected as architects because of their sympathy for art and their respect for Charles Harrison Townsend's workmanlike solution to the problem of bringing natural light to two floors of the original building. Gordon saw himself as a guardian of Townsend's simple, elegant gallery. The restraint of the Miller Colquhoun conversion (now considerably diminished by the most recent expansion to the gallery) owed everything to Colquhoun's stringent logic, coupled with Miller's facility for design, crucially tempered by Gordon's sympathetic critique.

More Boeing than Bauhaus

The principles of simplicity, straightforwardness, and absence of flourish governed all of Gordon's architectural work. In his own apartment, once memorably described as "more Boeing than Bauhaus," a series of chambers was separated from the external world by pulled white blinds, behind which he placed sleeved fluorescent tubes to give the impression of eternal daylight. All services and switches were hidden from view, and most objects cleared from every surface and placed out of sight behind white painted doors, long before such minimalist techniques became fashionable. At Boundary Road, the paint warehouse was turned into a space for art by his brilliant realization that in lowering the floor of the entrance gallery, he

"Ladder" by Joel Shapiro, at the Clocktower Gallery, New York, purchased by Gordon in 1973

would gain the height required to make this a grand, rather than oppressive, space. Equally original was his invention of troughs of "uplighters" that bounced light off the soffits to produce a constant source of light that appeared to come from the massive skylights, even at night. Such solutions, based on a deep understanding of the needs of art, were a product of an architectural mind that sought the traditional Palladian qualities of balance, purity, and calm. His projects may have looked effortless, but they were the product of his clear analysis of each brief, and his ability to establish elegant, logical plans drawn in characteristic freehand line, often overlaid with variations on tracing paper torn off a large roll. Later, his design associates would transform these into working drawings for the builder.

A major commission for a museum eluded him, though it might well have come but for his untimely death. Instead, his admirers in museums listened to his advice on which architects to employ, or engaged him as a consultant to act as a friendly critic of the local architect.

Gordon's Influence

In 1987, during the transformation of a vast nineteenth-century hospital building into the Museo Nacional Centro de Arte Reina Sofía in Madrid, founding director Carmen Gimenez asked Gordon to advise on the conversion of the spaces used for the initial exhibitions. Later, she selected him to lead a small committee with Edy de Wilde, the recently retired director of the Stedelijk Museum in Amsterdam, and me to advise the appointed architect on the conversion of the whole building. In an interview with art critic Michael Brenson in 2007, Gimenez recalled, "I have learned space from two essential people: Richard Serra and Max Gordon. Max was an animal of space, the same as Richard. They enter a space and immediately you can see they fill the space by the way they move. It's something you cannot explain."[2] As at Whitechapel, Gordon was a friendly scourge, the inquisitor whose disarmingly simple questions exposed any florid or superfluous intervention by the architect in the classical plan of the building. As a result, the simple vaulted beauty of the original ward rooms was preserved, and the Reina Sofía is widely admired for the elegant sequence of spaces in which artists and curators can make memorable installations. Later additions achieved without his controlling eye show how easily things can go wrong when architecture rather than art becomes the imperative. (See Chronology, pages 124–25.)

In London, the opening of Boundary Road in 1984 initiated developments that culminated in the opening of Tate Modern in 2000. Gordon's creation of a space for art that so cruelly exposed the limitations of the national museum's commitment to show contemporary art strengthened the voices of those seeking to change the accepted order. As so often before, the artists responded first. The pace was set by Damien Hirst and friends at Goldsmiths' College, where Craig-Martin, Richard Wentworth, and John Thomson were leading the advanced course. In 1988, inspired by the scale and ambition of Boundary Road and unknowingly adopting the model that had been proposed by Gordon for the King's Road show in 1973, they took over an empty warehouse in Docklands and presented the now legendary exhibition, *Freeze*. This was followed in quick succession by shows of equal ambition: *Modern Medicine*, *Gambler*, and finally, the *East Country Yard Show* in 1990. It was this activity, coupled with the success of Boundary Road, that in 1994 helped to lend credibility to a Tate proposal to convert the disused Bankside power station, glowering on the south side of the Thames opposite St. Paul's Cathedral, into the nation's museum of modern art.

An Exhibition Space for New Art

By that time a head of steam had been created at the Tate, led by a group of collectors who had formed the Patrons of New Art in 1982 and had established the Turner Prize in 1984. It is no surprise to discover that Gordon was also a prime mover on this front. Gordon was a member of the inaugural committee of the Patrons, a ginger group established to bring support, encouragement, and critical friendship to the Tate in showing developments in contemporary art. In a manuscript, presumably prepared for a meeting of the Patrons at Tate in late 1982, Gordon records in his clear, logical prose the steps required to establish "An Exhibition Space for New Art." He is sympathetic to the challenges facing a public museum. "The Tate

Robert Gober's "The Cut-Off Sink," 1985, was part of Gordon's collection

would like to avoid the unseemly antagonism aroused by the Carl Andre acquisition," he wrote, referring to the outcry that emerged upon the purchase and exhibition of the sculpture "Equivalent VII." However, he also comments, "so far, the placing of the [Julian] Schnabel and the [Jennifer] Bartlett exhibitions in two bays of the new extension has appeared physically pinched and tentative in purpose. There should be no reason, if conviction is there, why New Art should not seem to be as important as accepted and historic art."[3]

At the second meeting of the Patrons on November 30, 1982, the deadpan minutes record "item viii: Max Gordon suggested that the Patrons should establish an annual prize, sponsored by a large company, possibly in collaboration with Channel Four television, for achievement in the visual arts."[4] At one stroke, Gordon conceived the Turner Prize as we know it today, a prize that has brought international recognition to British art and to the Tate.

As this book demonstrates, Max Gordon was an architect with a rare gift for making spaces in which art takes precedence. He succeeded in following his own principles. "Everything possible must be done to allow the pictures to breathe and be enjoyed without distraction,"[5] he wrote for a lecture given in 1990. However, his lasting legacy lies not just in those spaces, but in the fruits of his ability to bring together artists, designers, collectors, and curators, and to cajole and inspire them into striving for more ambitious goals. His cosmopolitan attitude made him impatient with the traditional British excuses for not getting things done, or achieving them late, or in half-baked fashion. It was this drive that made him such a vital and witty companion and which ultimately gave him fulfillment as an architect. In the last nine years of his life Max Gordon created more superb and enduring spaces for art than many renowned architects manage in a lifetime. He also established a model for handling light and space that has been imitated but rarely equalled by countless others in creating galleries across the world.

Notes

1   Max Gordon Papers, TGA 9127, Tate Archive, London.
2   Michael Brenson, "In Conversation: Carmen Giménez with Michael Brenson," *The Brooklyn Rail*, July-August 2007.
3   Max Gordon Papers, PC 10.5, Tate Archive, London.
4   Patrons of New Art Committee, minutes, November 30, 1982, Tate Archive, London.
5   Max Gordon, "New Museum Architecture and Contemporary Art," 1990, Max Gordon Papers, TGA 9127/85, Tate Archive, London.

New Scotland Yard, which Gordon designed for Chapman, Taylor and Partners, 1962–66

Almost Nothing
Kenneth Frampton

Born in South Africa and educated at elite institutions around the world, Max Gordon was as much a culture diplomat and connoisseur as he was an architect. He was, in a very special sense of the term, a facilitator, a creator of situations, of contacts, scenes, and above all, an aficionado of art. It was this last overriding passion that determined the character of almost everything he did and it is this that explains the unique position he modestly occupied in the trajectory of contemporary architecture.

Mies van der Rohe's aphorism, *beinahe nichts*, ("almost nothing"), could well have been assumed by Max as a motto for practice, had he been inclined to do so. Hence, his affinity for Mies, or rather for SOM in their prime, for whom he worked from 1956 to 1962. This was Max Gordon's point of departure in architecture, even if there was barely a trace of Miesianism in his built work (apart from his habitual use of the MR chair). Max's "almost nothing" turned as much on artistic minimalism in general as on the minimalism of Mies. That is to say, it displayed a similar affinity for such diverse minimalists as Luis Barragan in architecture or James Turrell in art. From Gordon Bunshaft, for whom he worked at SOM, he must have acquired the idea that a mid-twentieth century architect must also, as part of his professional commitment, be both a connoisseur and a patron of modern art.

Possibly the most ambitious project of Max's career as a corporate architect was the New Scotland Yard office building (1962–66) on Victoria Street, London, which he designed while he was a partner in the practice of Chapman, Taylor and Partners. However, despite his passing enthusiasm for the modern project at a grand scale, when it came down to it, Max Gordon was not out to prove himself as a form-maker. On the contrary, he believed fervently in the opposite principle to such an extent that, at times, his work became almost invisible.

As far as his domestic practice was concerned he clearly subscribed to Barragan's edict that "an architecture that does not achieve tranquility fails in its spiritual mission." His own apartment at Mount Street in Mayfair was exemplary in this regard where, save for an overriding sense of comfort provided by a fitted carpet, everything else was reduced to a matter of light and proportion. Irrespective of whether the commission was public or private, everything turned for Max on contriving a subtly illuminated environment for art. As far as he was concerned, art alone was the guarantor of the essential plastic presence, energy, and significance for which architecture was merely the background.

It was this attitude that gained him the confidence of artists and art patrons alike and led to his ascendancy in the world of art rather than in architecture. Hence the residences that he designed for many artists and gallery owners on both sides of the Atlantic. In the last seven years of his life he received some major commissions, including the Boundary Road gallery for the Saatchi Collection, deftly inserted in the top-lit shell of a disused paint warehouse in St. John's Wood, London; the large exhibition sequence that he designed and lit for the Reina Sophía gallery in Madrid; and, finally, the posthumously completed Fisher Landau Center in Long Island City. One of the exceptions to Max's gallery practice was the Manilow residence, Chicago, of 1991, a classic modern house designed and executed with the utmost care and precision without any excess or a trace of spectacular pretension.

Apart from the mores of life itself, lived to the full, for Max Gordon there were two basic foci: the revered artwork from which everything radiated, and the small-scale tectonic detail that was in some way essential to the quality of light, the resonance of a surface, or the discretion of a trim to a door or a skirting. Artificial

light was a particular penchant and it led to a number of ingenious devices, bordering on inventions, such as his booster trough-lighting or the fluorescent Synskin light column, illuminated from within by twin fluorescent tubes that remained invisible due to the shade's opacity. The placement of such diffused light columns in window reveals was intended to augment the ambient light and to compensate for the absence of natural light at night.

In his lifetime, Max Gordon played many roles—impresario, raconteur, curator, cultural diplomat—but he was, in the end, first and last, an architect in the service of art.

Mies van der Rohe's Crown Hall, 1955–56, on the Illinois Institute of Technology campus, Chicago

Major Works

120 Mount Street

98a Boundary Road

Brody House

Annely Juda Fine Art

Sachs House

Manilow House

Fisher Landau Center for Art

120 Mount Street

London, 1977–1981

Doris Lockhart Saatchi

When Max Gordon found the Victorian attic in Mayfair that became his top-floor flat, it was just the combination of cramped rooms, ungainly corridors, clumsy moldings, and mean fireplaces he'd been looking for. Such an architectural hodgepodge presented the ideal opportunity to make the changes he wanted with a free hand and a clear professional conscience. In less than a year, a cluttered space once occupied only by parlor maids and steamer trunks became a spacious aerie of white walls, cream carpet, minimal furniture, diffused light, and elegant works of art.

It's not altogether surprising that Max's apartment seemed to have a transatlantic air about it. In a year at Harvard's Graduate School of Design, he developed a taste for open spaces, a preference for rational design, and a flair for simple solutions that most people think of as particularly American. These proclivities have distinguished his work, from an early indoor swimming pool for a private house in Buckinghamshire to plans for a marina at Brighton. His brief to himself as architect from himself as client was simple: "a quiet space." So much of his carefully drawn-up budget went to "making the place look straightforward," to achieving the effect of no effect.

Max described his flat with amusement as "soft tech," but a serious look reveals some well thought-out and firmly held principles of design, ideas that are adamantly opposed to many traditional concepts. He had, for instance, an abhorrence of corridors: "They are an English disease. To walk through a corridor to get from one room to another seems absolutely crazy." So he did away with them in his flat, in the process doing away with almost all the dividing walls to leave a nearly open space and, at its core, a stately ship-like funnel containing the building's main stairwell and elevator. "In the back of my mind, I rather wanted it to be like room settings in the furniture department of Bloomingdale's, where you just flow from one to the other."

By the same reasoning he also got rid of all but one of the fireplaces. "Normally, people who don't have a fireplace put one in, then gear the room around it. Along with doors and windows, it's a primary consideration in an English home. I've just changed the rules to avoid being locked in that situation. I've obliterated the fireplaces, I don't have doors because this is all one space, and I've obliterated the windows." Max somehow had to screen his badly overlooked windows from the outside world. So he installed wall-to-wall, ceiling-to-floor sliding panels made of a fiberglass material available at the time only in the U.S. as filters in batteries and known as "Synskin." A simple and cheap solution if ever there was one, it can be cut to size with a pair of scissors, and the fibers repel dirt. The panels screened both daylight and the light from fluorescent tubes installed in the window wells, providing evenly diffused lighting throughout the flat. They also hid radiators, wall plugs, electrical wires, a TV set, and stereo units, and smoothed out one or two awkward jogs in the exterior walls—a perfect example of Max's talent for simplification down to the smallest detail.

To gain wall space, doors were jibbed, fitted flush to the walls with no frames or moldings, as they are on a ship. Simple aluminum ship's hinges and latches were fitted in the bathroom and on cupboard doors. Plain white vinyl covered the walls and the bathroom floor. The apparently artless sofa and seating units, designed by Max and made by the British luxury brand Asprey, seemed like comfortable "mounds on the floor."

Gordon's dressing room

For a large number of guests, he pushed his bed out of the way and into the dressing room through a hinged flap; for houseguests he pushed his huge armless and backless seating units together into a generous bed. His other furniture was made up of classic pieces he had for years, like the Corbusier chaise longue and Mies van der Rohe table and stool, or interesting ad-libs, like the desk top made from the backing that keeps Formica from warping, or a steel medical trolley that served as a rolling side table for drinks or party food.

As a fledgling architect in America, Max also developed a passion for contemporary art. He couldn't afford Rothkos, Pollocks, or Newmans, so he began looking at young, relatively unknown artists and bought their work early. By the early 1980s he had one of the most adventurous collections of contemporary art in England, although only a part of it was in the flat at any one time. One month a tiny ladder sculpture by Joel Shapiro would rise mysteriously against the wall next to a grid of metal plates painted systematically with prim black dots by Jennifer Bartlett. Another month a talismanic wall sculpture by John Duff might have loomed opposite a four-panel painting on parchment-like sections by Stephen Buckley. A reticent three-part work by Tony Carter faced an exuberant construction by Rick Stich.

Again and again, talking about his flat, Max would express his admiration for the American way of doing things: "The attitude is what I like more than any particular style. People are much more nonchalant about things and at the same time more audacious. They just do it, and do it very effortlessly and gracefully." Though he was far too modest ever to do so, Max might have been describing the way he worked. It's worth noting, however, that even a farseeing and sensitive architect working for himself is capable of a minor misjudgment. Max said he kept one of the fireplaces because he thought it might be nice to have a fire from time to time. "I never have had one," he said. The realization came as a surprise and made him laugh.

Previously published in *World of Interiors*, September 1982.

The cylindrical elevator shaft sat in the middle of the main live-work area. Matt Rugg's "Smoke Stack," 1966, center.

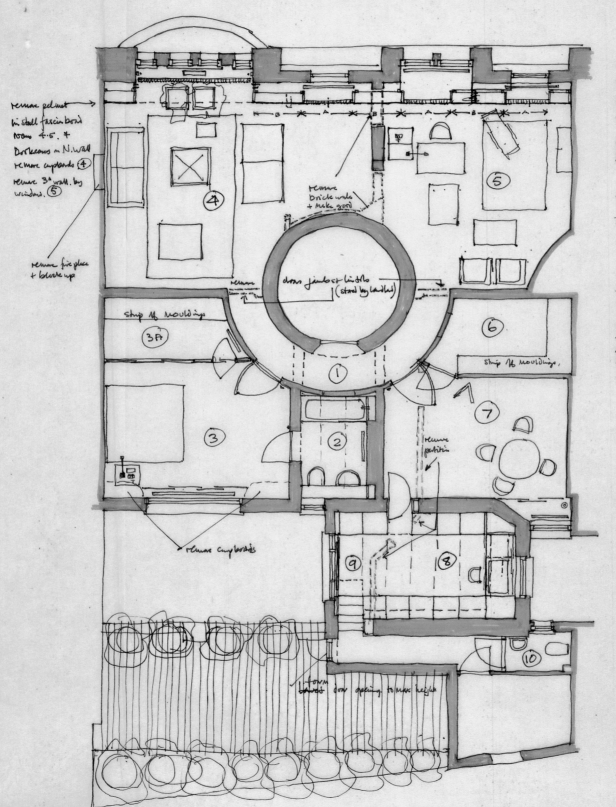

remove pelmet
install fascia board
rooms 4.5. +
Dormers on N. wall
remove cupboards ④
remove 3rd wall. by
windows ⑤

remove fireplace
+ block up

Strip off mouldings
③A

remove cupboards

remove
brick wall
+ make good

doors jambs+ lintels
(stood by builder)

remove

Strip off mouldings

remove partition

form lower door opening to max. height

Cornices at ceilings removed
+ made good. Rooms ③④⑤

Remove timber mouldings from
walls + make good ④⑤ Rooms

fill in skirting groove. ④⑤
flush with wall

Room 2.
ceiling use prosper panels
from Belgrave Sq.
false floor. (timber).
install bathroom suite (new)
cut back step on Room 3 side
provide ventation vent unit
tiles round bath only.

Room 3A + 3A.
form walls in cupboard with
timber stud partition with jibbed
door.

120 MOUNT ST 5TH floor
Louis de Soissons Partnership
7314| P. 16
1:50. 11 March 1977

N

Opposite: Early plan showing walls in red, most of which were removed in the final design

Above: View from living area toward the study, with Synskin lighting on the windows at left, and John Duff's "Untitled," 1973, on the round wall

Above left: View from the dining area to the custom-built bookcase. Ron Gorchov's "Blue Piece," 1972, in the foreground.

Above right: Italian dining table made of grained wood and alumninum, Thonet Vienna chairs, bookcase, and Rick Stich's "Oaxaca Tornadoes," 1975

Opposite: A jib door, flanked by artwork, led from the bedroom to bathroom

Above: Living area with a Mies van der Rohe table and antique Balinese puppets. Stephen Buckley's "Fresh End," 1971, above the sofa.

Opposite: View into the master bedroom. A folding screen designed by Gordon offered the only privacy from the rest of the apartment. Keith Milow's "First Drawing Five," 1973, hung over the bed.

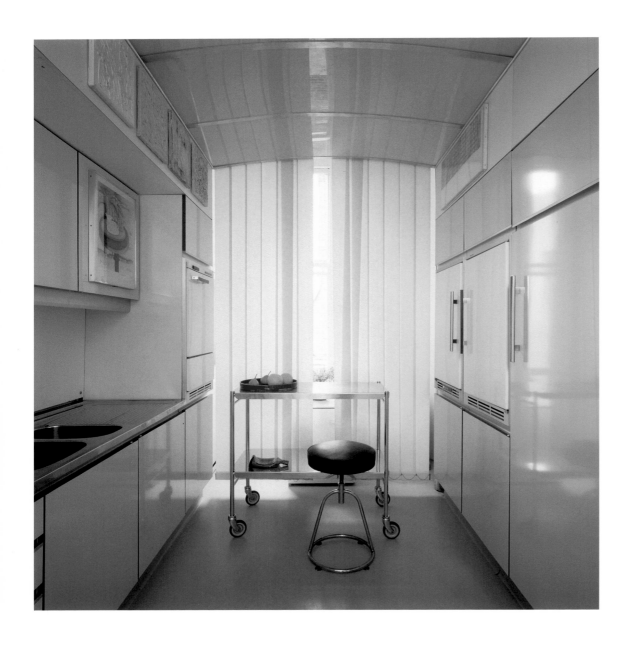

Above: Kitchen, with rolling steel cart

Opposite: The simplicity and clean lines of the bathroom evoked the efficiency of an airplane or ship lavatory

98a Boundary Road

London, 1983–1985

Doris Lockhart Saatchi

When, in 1983, Charles and I discovered the disused, former paint distribution warehouse that was to become the Boundary Road home of the original Saatchi collection, there was never any question about our choice of architect to convert it to a space for the enjoyment of the artworks that we were so obsessively acquiring. Max Gordon was one of only a handful of people in London, maybe even in Britain, who knew and liked the art that we found so exciting and desirable, most of which was part of the surge of creative energy that was happening in New York at the time.

From the outside, as we walked around it, the building seemed promising: a discreet, gated site behind a row of two-story neighborhood shops; no windows; room for big art-bearing trucks to enter and turn and back up to a loading bay; and best of all, a glazed, sawtooth roof that provided top lighting.

So we got the keys and invited Max to come along and have a look. Inside, the building was almost too good to be true: 30,000 square feet of column-free, open space, thanks to the use of long-span steel trusses in its construction. With Max, you always knew he was thinking hard about something when he went silent. Max went silent. Finally, he said, "It's great."

"There's just one problem," we said. "The ceilings aren't high enough, and you can't raise the roof." "We'll dig down," said Max. And that was it. The contractors dug and dug some more and then they hit water. "Don't worry," said Max, "we'll waterproof the excavation." There was a delay, but we got the ceiling height we needed in an enormous space that could accommodate monumental works by artists such as Richard Serra, Donald Judd, and Anselm Kiefer.

Max manipulated the space, as he always did, so that it looked as if it couldn't have been arranged any other way. The "rooms" he formed never appeared forced or awkward and flowed naturally from one to the next. At Boundary Road, he created five galleries, each with its own character.

Visitors entered the building at street level, where a reception area contained a desk, restrooms, a small office, and enough wall and floor space to install a few artworks that served to introduce the exhibition within. Much as Frank Lloyd Wright designed compressed entry areas that open into generously proportioned spaces and give them greater impact, Max lowered the ceiling, then presented the visitor with stairs down into the enormous, high-walled Gallery One. With its glazed, sawtooth roof open to the sky and daylight, it became an amphitheater where visitors stepping into it became not just bystanders but part of the drama of the exhibition itself.

At one end of Gallery One, stairs ran the full width of the generous opening to Gallery Two, where Max retained the sawtooth (sometimes called dogtooth) roof but left the floor at its original level. There the space was less theatrical, a somewhat conventional gallery carved out of an industrial building. To the left was an opening that led to a more compact space, Gallery Five, which eventually contained only one permanently installed work of art, the mentally indelible "20:50" by Richard Wilson. The reflection of the glass panes of the roof on the motionless and shiny surface of black oil created a sense of disorientation, a ripple of confusion in the visitor who stood, seemingly perilously, on a constructed parapet half-submerged in the dangerous and threatening viscous liquid.

Entry to the gallery

Back in the safety of Gallery Two, openings in the opposite wall led to the calm of Galleries Three and Four, both modest and artificially lit spaces, where Max installed a lowered ceiling to better accommodate smaller, more intimate works and shield vulnerable works, such as drawings, from daylight.

Never was there a trace of sensationalism or self-advertisement in Max's designs. Instead, he skillfully used the simplest, and often least expensive, means to achieve calm and beautiful effects. He started at Boundary Road by painting the reconfigured interior white, down to every nut, bolt and washer. He then specified a poured concrete floor and had it painted a soft gray color. Simplicity itself. Yet he also developed ideas that, at the time, seemed revolutionary in spaces designed for the display of works of art. For example, other architects who were far more famous than Max quickly adopted his ingenious lighting system of simple, white-painted metal troughs that carried lighting tubes. Unseen from the floor and aimed at the ceiling, they created reflected light that bathed the spaces below and the works in them with an even, shadow-free luminosity.

Familiar with the needs of spaces for the presentation of contemporary art, Max also designed in a thoroughly practical way. At Boundary Road he marked out a four-foot corridor between the outer walls of the building and the inner studding walls, where artworks could be stored, studding could be reinforced for especially heavy pieces, and electric cables could be run to where they were needed. "No Trim," a note that appeared on one of his many drawings and some of his seemingly casual sketches, was Max's guiding principle, and he assiduously forewent all the architectural niceties, such as baseboards and architraves, that many architects of his day seemed unable to leave out of their designs. Max could be said to have perfected the white box art space that is still, for many, the best environment for contemporary art.

Unlike so many architects then and now, Max made comfortable homes for often "difficult" art, just as he made comfortable living spaces for the complicated lives of his collector friends and clients. He was the rare practitioner who was able to resist the pressure of great modernist architects like Mies van der Rohe, who made good walls and enclosures in his buildings, but not good walls for paintings or good enclosures for sculpture.

Of course, Max's fine plans for Boundary Road did have a couple of shortcomings. I had to insist on an extra cubicle in the women's restrooms, for example. "Oh, all right then," said a much amused Max, humoring me in his best, big-daddy manner. I also argued hard for disabled access, which wasn't at that time required by law, but even Max couldn't figure out how to provide for that in a simple and aesthetically pleasing way.

Recently, I went back to see what had become of the building that Max transformed into one of the most admired contemporary art spaces in the world. The entrance to the site was, for almost two decades, indicated only by a dove gray metal gate, and a post discretely marked "98a" has been replaced by a heavily varnished timber door studded with garish, colored glass panels. The building is gone, and the place that helped give the British public a taste for the pleasures and pranks of contemporary art and encouraged a bunch of bright young British artists of the day to make the most exciting work anywhere is now a gated enclave of polite brick houses named, as the brass letters on the door proudly proclaim, "The Collection."

Adapted excerpt from a book of memoirs that Doris Lockhart Saatchi is writing entitled *In My View*.

Above: The interior prior to Gordon's intervention

Opposite: Paintings by Andy Warhol hang in Gallery Two; beyond, in Gallery One, Donald Judd sculptures and the steps to the reception area

Charles Saatchi

Max Gordon was unique among architects in wanting to make the presentation of artworks more important than displaying the talents of the architect. He immediately understood that a 30,000-square-foot building on Boundary Road in London, once the storage depot for a paint distributor, could be turned into a dramatic showcase for art by highlighting the scale and utilizing the overhead natural light of the building.

He brilliantly decided to drop the floor level by five feet in order to generate extra height and created five well-proportioned gallery rooms, with all storage requirements hidden out of sight behind the gallery walls. He also created a simple heating system that kept the galleries warm in winter, without any intrusive vents. The lighting was an innovative line of suspended white trays, holding fluorescent lights pointing upwards at the skylights. The vast galleries were given an airy feeling of natural light at all times through these trays, held high just below the ceiling rafters, bouncing the light off the ceiling in an unobtrusive, almost invisible way.

Max was a wonderfully kind and gentle man, who wore his intelligence and sophistication lightly. I miss his company a great deal, and wish he were still here to help make our gallery better, though I try to remember all the invaluable lessons he taught me.

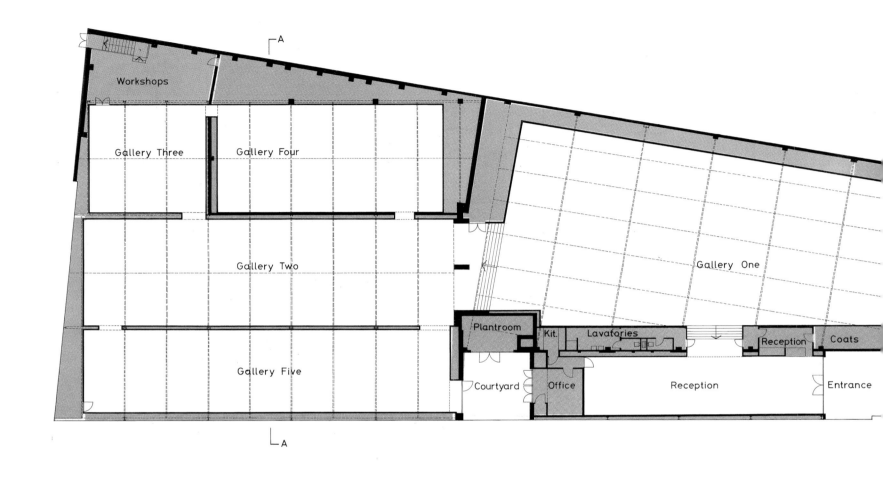

Workshops

Gallery Three

Gallery Four

Gallery Two

Gallery One

Gallery Five

Plantroom

Kit.

Lavatories

Reception

Coats

Courtyard

Office

Reception

Entrance

Previous spread: Sol LeWitt, "Wall Drawing No. 273," 1975, and "Serial Project I (A, B, C, D)", 1966, in Gallery One

Clockwise from top left: Plan; section through Gallery One looking toward Reception; section through Reception and Gallery One; section of Galleries Four, Two, and Five

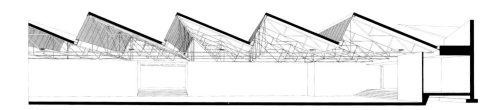

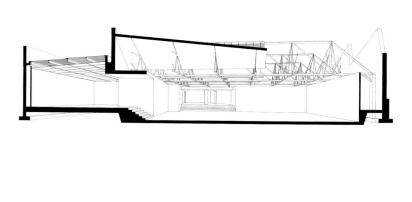

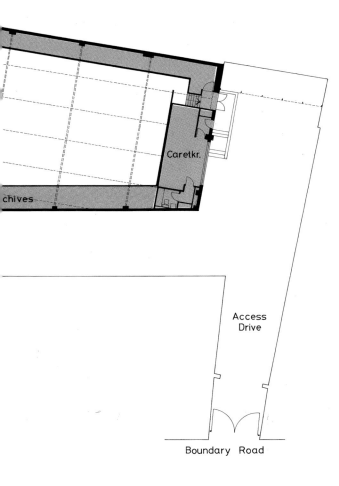

Caretkr.

chives

Access
Drive

Boundary Road

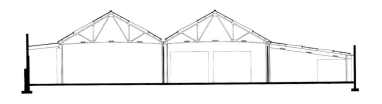

Above: Works by Robert
Ryman in Gallery Two

Opposite: Donald Judd sculptures displayed in Gallery One,
with stairs leading to Reception
at right

Above: Richard Wilson's site-specific installation, "20:50," 1987, a steel tank of used sump oil with a walkway, in Gallery Five

Opposite: The sloped roof of Gallery Five could still accommodate large sculptures, like these by Richard Serra, before "20:50" was permanently installed

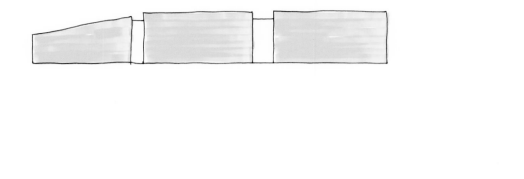

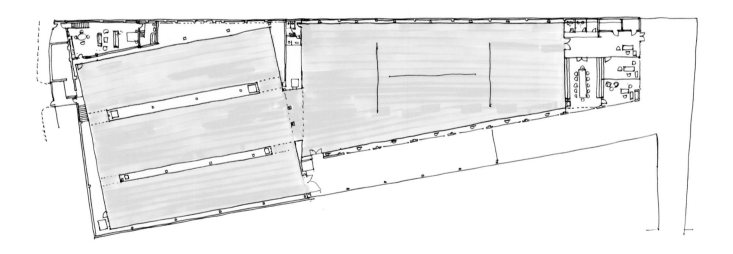

Opposite: The reception gallery
with Richard Serra's "Kitty
Hawk," 1983

Above: Freehand elevations
and plan

Brody House

New York, 1987–1990

Jackie Brody

My husband Gene and I met Max Gordon for the first time on October 30, 1987. We had just contracted to buy a 120-year-old townhouse in New York City's Upper East Side and needed an architect to plan extensive renovations. We wanted to keep a sense of the past, retaining the house's special New York charm, but letting in light and space. Max had done that at the Brooke Alexander Gallery in Soho, where I loved to see prints in the small, square viewing room he had designed. He visited the house that day, asked for our ideas, and then toured our apartment, opening closets and drawers to see how we lived.

One week later Max presented us with plans for all five floors and the basement. We had changed our minds about the location of the master bedroom. He left us with tracing paper so we could note other changes we might like. There were a few, always accommodated, but the house, completed shortly before his death in 1990, is basically the design he first gave us.

The house was full of small rooms on each floor. He took down as many walls as possible so that light would flood in from both ends. On the first floor he kept the garage, a rare New York feature that had attracted us to the house in the first place, added a foyer, and created an open kitchen facing the garden. On the second floor he created fine spaces for viewing art in a square dining room and a living room looking out over the garden. Removing layers uncovered the original high ceiling and dentil moldings in the dining room. In the living room, he placed outlets and radiators inconspicuously in the newly stained black floor to avoid distracting attention away from the fine architectural details of the 1920s.

On the third floor he gave our bedroom two bathrooms and an open sitting area, clearing an unobstructed space from the front windows to back. Gene used to sit in the Eames chair at night and read by the warm light coming from behind the Synskin blinds. On the fourth floor, Max made the offices for our publication, the *Print Collector's Newsletter*, with four desks, a wall of bookshelves and a dramatic nine-window grid between the office and stairwell. I insisted on a white floor for the office. Max was dubious. Since he was such a visual person, I took him to see the studio of our friends Stephen and Naomi Antonakos, who had used a tough white enamel paint on their floors. Max was enchanted. On the smaller top floor he made a small self-contained studio.

Max understood from his knowledge of London townhouses how to maximize the use of space. There were bookshelves on three floors, all with matching two-inch shelving, for our many books of all kinds. We put in an elevator that went to the top but meant that space had to be given up on each floor. The stairwell was originally rectangular, but Max built false curved walls that played off the existing curved handrail and hid the electric wiring. In the stairway he created illuminated niches, whose shapes were inspired by the living-room cornice. Two enlarged and squared skylights let in yet more light.

He was amused that I wanted to bring all my old furniture into this new house, but he found space for the white Vignelli Saratoga sofas, black leather and steel Wassily chairs by Breuer, and the Mies van der Rohe cantilever chair. He introduced me to de Sede sofas; he liked the shape, I liked the fact that they could be turned into beds for guests.

Max encouraged us to recycle hardware and fixtures from the past and to research new materials and sources. Sometimes he chose from samples; more often he went with me to showrooms, from the city's fanciest to Bowery restaurant suppliers. If we could not find anything that pleased us, he'd say, "I'll have to design something." And he would, whether lightworks for the stairway, bathroom mirrors, kitchen trolleys, chopping boards, or end tables. We managed to retain nearly all the old plumbing fixtures and fittings. I wanted a Japanese-style metal bathtub. We went to industrial suppliers but in the end Max designed one, and made sure that it had insulation to avoid hollow sounds.

He stayed with us all the way, from demolition through the installation of furniture. It was not always easy. "Jackie, you must have standards," he would say. The house included some signature Gordonisms, like the Synskin columns of light. Other designs he created for us, like the deep kitchen counter he repeated in the Manilow House or the sliding dining room panels he adapted for the Fisher Landau Center for Art. He made us part of his lexicon and his legacy—the result of a rare response to architectural problems and respect for others, even clients.

The office contained furniture by Ron Arad (bottom left), and Eero Aarnio (bottom right)

The parlor floor, or second floor, contained the living and dining rooms. Ellsworth Kelly's "White Brown," 1968, hangs on the left. Mies van der Rohe chairs and an Eero Saarinen dining table bask in diffused Synskin light.

Opposite: Staircase with
Synskin niche cutout in false
curved wall

Above: Niche detail

Above: The third-floor sitting room with custom-designed shelves and Kenneth Snelson's sculpture, "Osaka," 1969, in front of the fireplace

Opposite left: The sitting room contained a chair and ottoman (foreground) designed by Gordon

Opposite right: The third-floor master bedroom. The bedside table was designed by Gordon; Peter Shire's "Kandissy's Red Dot" chair, 1986, bottom right.

Above: Gordon left the original
second-floor fireplace and
architectural details

Opposite: Vignelli Saratoga
sofas in the living room

Annely Juda Fine Art

London, 1989–1990

David Juda

My mother, Annely Juda, was the doyenne of modern and contemporary art dealers in London, opening her first gallery in 1960. Before that she worked for the collector and eventual gallerist Eric Estorick and through him met Max's mother, Tania Gordon. Tania began to paint in her fifties, eschewing any formal training, and Estorick gave her encouragement. Annely got to know Max independently as one of a group of friends that included the artists and theater designers Nicholas Georgiadis and Barry Kay.

Annely Juda Fine Art opened in an industrial building in Tottenham Mews, off Charlotte Street, in 1968, before it became fashionable to repurpose such buildings. When new space was found on the top floor of another industrial building on Dering Street, off New Bond Street, in August 1989, Annely and I asked Max to come and take a look before signing the lease.

I remember Max walking around the space. It had been a sweatshop, where ball gowns were made and altered, and was very messy. Within a few minutes Max drew the basic plan on the inside of a cigarette pack. I questioned whether the partition for the office should be on the other side of a beam. Max said no, and it turned out that he was right.

The gallery showed sculpture as well as paintings and drawings. David Nash and Anthony Caro are both gallery artists. How would we get large sculptures up to a fourth-floor space? Max asked us to specify the maximum likely dimension and weight of sculptures that had to be brought in. The answer: an eight-foot cube and two tons. Max designed a gantry crane to sit on the roof that could lift a load from street level, travel it a few feet inward, and then deposit it through a sliding roof skylight and into the gallery. Once planning permission had been obtained for the crane, the building work started, and the gallery opened in June 1990.

The gallery also acquired the third floor of the building for storage. Max designed trap doors in the floors so that sculpture could be brought down to it. Max worked with his usual collaborator in Britain, Richard Goldsbrough. We subsequently acquired the second floor for gallery space and Goldsbrough replicated the trap doors so that artworks could be easily placed on any of our three floors. The sliding skylight, made by a Danish firm, is on runners, works perfectly, and has never leaked.

Max positioned the offices so that Annely and I were near the reception desk. While there was a certain amount of privacy, people we knew could wander in for a chat, and we could keep half an eye on comings and goings. Our desks faced each other so that we could be kept easily informed of what we were both doing. Annely died in 2006, and I am now running the gallery.

The gantry crane was installed on the roof to lower artwork into the gallery

Views of the main gallery
space with paintings by
Prunella Clough

The main gallery's skylight provides abundant natural light for exhibitions, and slides open to allow the gantry crane to lower large artworks into the space

Above: Anthony Caro's
"Cretan Passage," 2005/07,
in the main gallery

Opposite: Fourth-floor
gallery plan

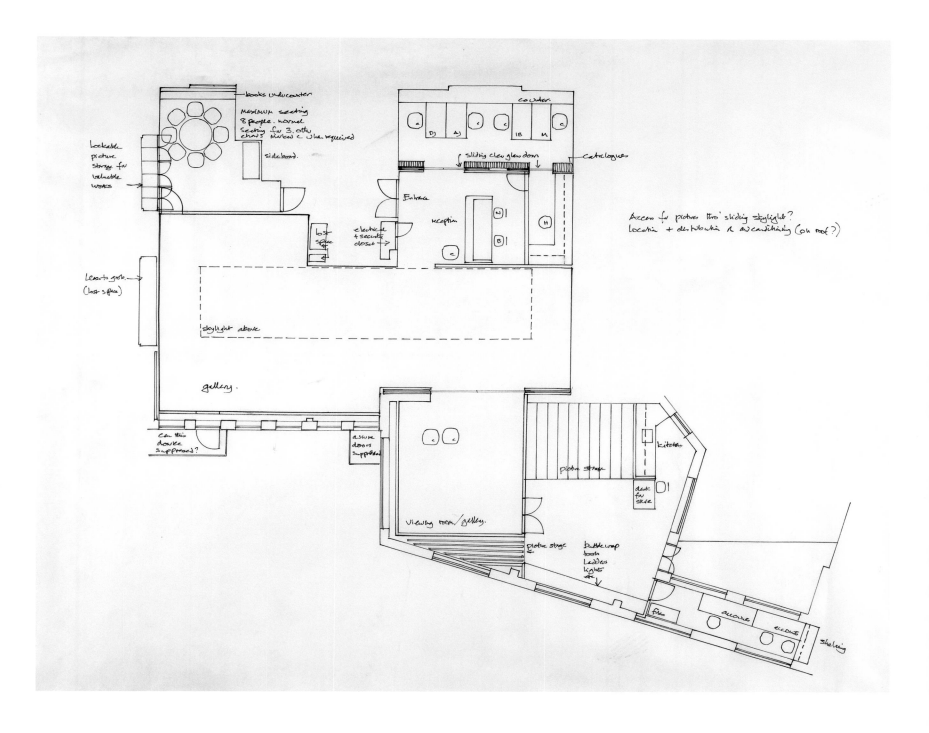

books undercounter
MAXIMUM seating
8 people. normal
Seating for 3. other
chairs Mixed c when required
Lockable picture storage for valuable works
sideboard.
counter.
sliding clear glass down
catalogues
Entrance
reception
Access for pictures thro' sliding skylight?
Location + distribution of air conditioning (on roof?)
lost space
electrical + security closet
Leanto garb.
(lost space)
skylight above
gallery.
Can this double suppressed?
assume doors suppressed
viewing room/gallery.
picture storage
kitchen
desk for store
picture storage
bubble wrap
tools
Ladders
lights
etc
files
allowance
allowance
shelving

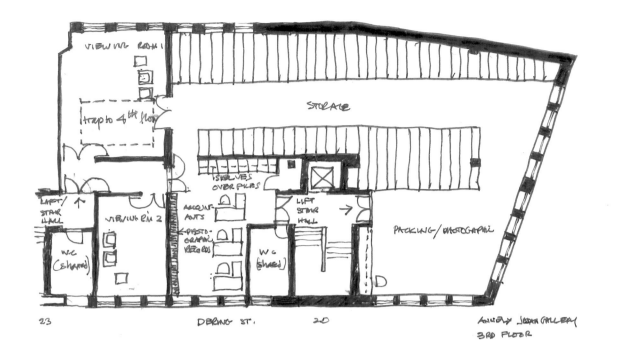

VIEWING ROOM 1

trap to 4th floor

STORAGE

SHELVES
OVER PILES

LIFT/
STAIR
HALL

VIEWING RM 2

ACCOUNT-
ANTS

PHOTO-
GRAPHIC
RECORDS

LIFT
STAIR
HALL

PACKING/PHOTOGRAPH

WC
(shared)

WC
(shared)

WC
(shared)

23

DERING ST.

20

ANNELY JUDA GALLERY
3RD FLOOR
20/23 DERING ST W1
MAX GORDON ASSOCIATES
FEB. 18. 1990.

Above: The third floor contains
office and storage space

Opposite: The drop-floor
leads down to the third floor.
Installed is a 2002 exhibition
of Edwina Leapman paintings.

Sachs House

Philadelphia, 1989–1990

Keith and Kathy Sachs

We live in a large house outside Philadelphia. By the mid-1980s we were running out of space to install art, and we didn't have the wall space to install big pieces such as those being made by German artists like Anselm Kiefer and Sigmar Polke. Our thought, as non-architects, was to build a satellite space. We talked about our ideas to two artist friends, Howard Hodgkin and Richard Serra, and both of them said: call Max Gordon.

We did not know Max then, but certainly knew of him. He had a pretty big reputation in the art world because of the Saatchi Gallery at Boundary Road, which we had seen. Would he consider our project?

We did not want a gallery down the hall, away from the living space of the house. Nor did Max. He didn't want the art to be something that you visited; he wanted the art to be something that you lived with. He came to visit and identified a large space right under our feet. It was a family room that had been constructed six years earlier. It was within the flow of the house, between the living and dining rooms. He said, "We're going to knock down the family room and take in part of the garden. My big challenge will be to give you back a space in which you could actually live among the art." He took that aspect of the project very seriously.

The room he designed was large: forty by forty feet. Max was very conscious of how this addition would relate to the rest of the house, not just from the inside, but from the outside. He didn't want it to look like an appendage, but to blend into the original house. Max worked with our landscape architect, Owen Schmidt, who was then more than eighty years old.

Max installed two steel beams to support the roof so that there would be no columns. This meant there would be a flat roof, and our bedroom above would look out over this huge flat surface. Our real estate agent said that an important factor in a resale would be a splendid master bedroom. That clicked with us and with Max, so that's what led to the building of a new master bedroom and bath upstairs on top of the big room, eliminating the resale problem completely.

The doors go all the way to the ceiling, which is very tall at twelve feet. Max did not want a transom above them. He wanted everything to open as high as possible. They were made out of wood in Vermont. They have worked perfectly.

Max was very exacting: he wanted that sixteenth-of-an-inch reveal at the bottom of the wall. The builders responded to the challenge. They became the keepers of the flame. Sometimes the architect of record, the Klett Organization, was very protective, but the builders said, "We think we can do this!"

The spirit of Max is very alive in the room. Max always made you laugh, always made you feel good. It was a joyous experience to work with him because he was so very good, so precise in what he envisioned.

Exterior view looking into the forty-by-forty-foot living room designed by Gordon

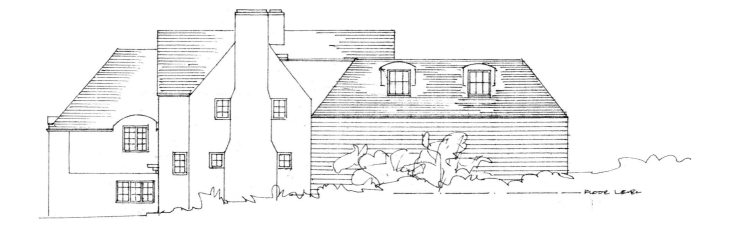

FLOOR LEVEL

Above: South elevation, showing the new room at right

Opposite: Twelve-foot-high
doors allow for ample natural
light

The room was designed to accommodate both large works of art and functional living room furniture. Anselm Kiefer's "Saturnzeit," 1986, Donald Judd's "Untitled," 1989, and Sigmar Polke's "Bei den Samojeden," 1988, hang on the wall from left to right.

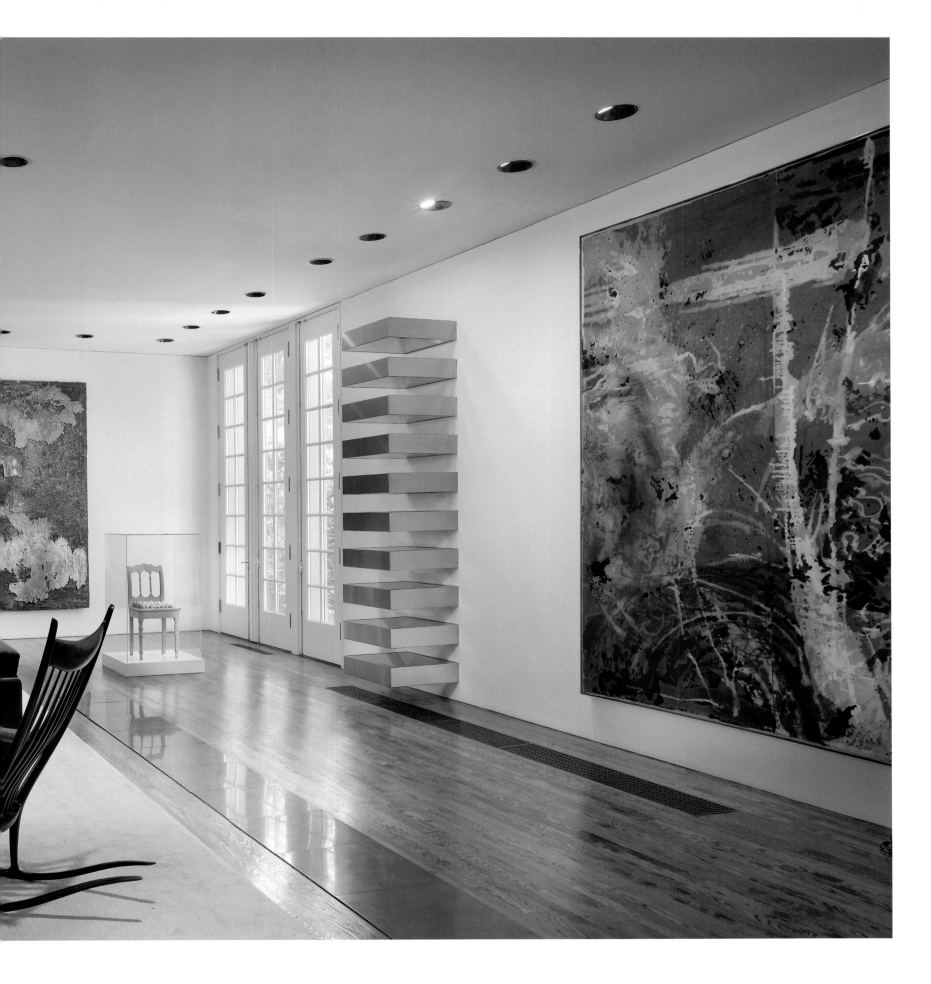

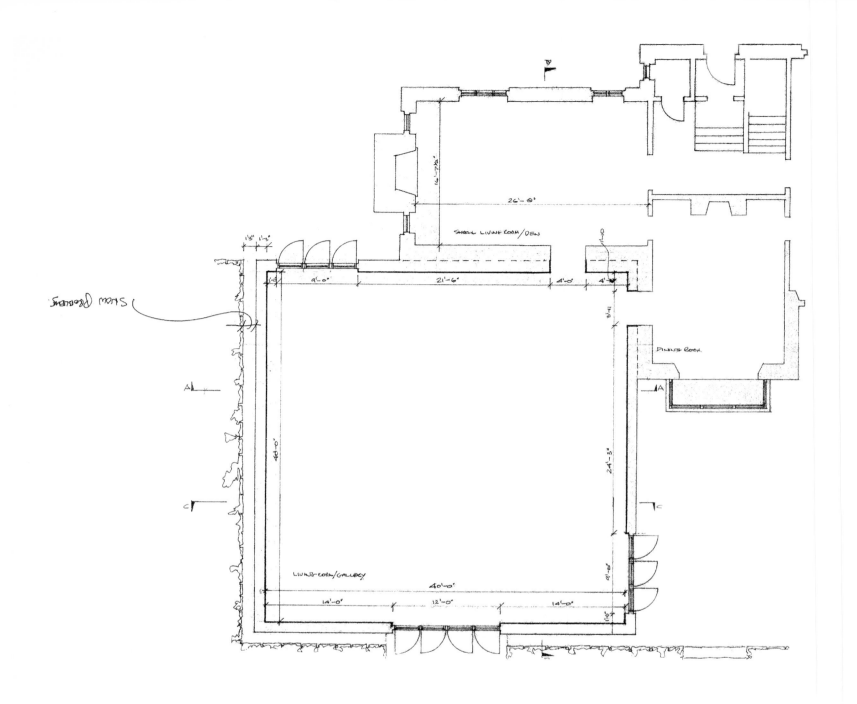

Show Reveals

Small living room/den

26'-0"

16'-7½"

Dining Room

1'-0"

40'-0"

24'-3"

9'-0"

21'-6"

4'-0"

4'

9'-0"

1'-0"

Living room/gallery

40'-0"

14'-0"

12'-0"

14'-0"

1'-0"

1'-3" 1'-3"

Above: Ground floor plan

Opposite: Gordon dictated a sixteenth-of-an-inch reveal between the floor and the wall. Joel Shapiro's sculpture, "Untitled," 1989–90, is anchored to the floor.

Above: Gordon created a
room that was comfortable
and inviting, where the Sachs
could enjoy their contemporary
art collection. "Yellow Relief
with White," by Ellsworth Kelly,
1990, hangs on the right wall.

Opposite: Tim Hawkinson's
sculpture, "Sherpa," 2008,
in the foreground, and Brice
Marden's "Red Ground Letter,"
2007–10, in the background

Manilow House

Chicago, 1989–1992

Lewis and Susan Manilow

We met Max in 1980 while visiting his apartment near the Connaught Hotel in London with a group from the Museum of Contemporary Art, Chicago. That night we also met and became friends with Charles and Doris Saatchi. This led to dinner with Charles, Doris, and Max every time we were in London.

The next year, Susan made the astonishing suggestion that we build a house. Equally astonishing was my immediate agreement, even though neither of us had ever owned a house, nor had any of our parents. We could create spaces and ceiling heights to accommodate much of our contemporary art collection, I could work at home, and Susan could have a patio and the garden of her dreams. In sum, we only needed the architect and the site in order to build a home tailored to our art and our lives.

We had scheduled a lunch with Max. The night before, I turned to Susan and said, "How about Max for our architect?" She hesitated about ten seconds and said, "Of course." We had seen Max's design for Boundary Road in London and a number of galleries in New York City. But even more important, we felt instinctively that Max shared our vision and would design the right building for us and our collection.

Over lunch I told Max we were planning to sell our apartment and wanted him to design our home. He responded, "How can you sell that apartment? It's my favorite in the world." Susan then outlined her vision: a U-shaped house facing south for sun, with a patio inside the U and an adjacent garden. Max accepted the commission and asked us to hire a local architect to handle detail drawings, permits, and on-site supervision. As we left, I asked Max if he had ever built a house before, and the answer seemed to be "no." However, that did not deter us in the least.

A month or so later Max stayed in our apartment, and we introduced him to John Vinci, Chicago's leading preservationist, who is also a modernist architect, having studied under Mies van der Rohe. We also knew that John had installed art exhibitions for major museums. Max and John got along famously.

In the meantime, we began our search for the site. Luck was with us when one evening, leaving an art dealer's home on Howe Street, Susan said, "There's a sign—four lots for sale, 100 x 125 foot frontage." We bought the property, which had once been a church, now divided into two apartments.

Max went back to London and started designing our new house. We received Max's first design, a rectangular plan, explaining that he couldn't provide an adequate space for the art within the U. I wrote back, "Not acceptable, try again."

Shortly after, a design appeared for a U-shaped house facing south, with a modest front on the street side, as we wished, and an extension to the west for the kitchen, garage, and another bedroom. We were overjoyed, and Max and John began to turn the sketches into plans for the contractor.

Exterior eastern view from the street

Susan defined the basic premises: natural light, real plaster, common Chicago brick, eight-inch-wide planks on the first floor, and a living room to accommodate very large pictures, including Anselm Kiefer's eighteen-foot-wide "Jerusalem." Max added one-foot-square tiles on the kitchen wall.

Max took the opportunity to buy Czech & Speake bathroom fixtures, a bow to England, at Chicago's Merchandise Mart. We discussed at length the library-dining room, situated between the living room and the kitchen, and decided that it should have books on all three sides and that the bookcases should be similar to those in Chareau's Maison de Verre in Paris. But this wonderful library meant that we had inadequate space for art. Max immediately responded, designing an entire skylit gallery on top of the living room—a crucial addition.

But probably his most popular and dramatic installation were the unique lights in the window frames on the first floor. Max designed two huge windows facing the patio and the nearly floor-to-ceiling doors that were manufactured and installed by Hope's Windows. Max's lighting design in the adjacent walls was deceptively simple, consisting of fluorescent tubes covered by a special scrim, making the light appear incandescent. Whenever we had visitors, we would show off this extraordinary lighting to their astonishment.

Construction was fast-tracked, meaning we were digging foundations while designing the next phase. We didn't actually have a budget, but selected three or four of the best contractors and evaluated their bids and capabilities. We were living in our new home a mere twenty-five months after our decision to build one.

Max, John, and Susan made a great team, and my role was mainly to oversee the finances and see that we had enough space for our art. I did request, however, a modest exterior without a high fence, which was agreeable to all. In only two instances did I override Max's plans. The first was to demand a basement. Max assented and designed one large enough for a small gallery. The second was more complicated. Max had designed an excellent closet for our bedroom, but it was large enough for only one person. There was no other space for a second closet, but Max once again accommodated by extending a small space over the kitchen. It was difficult for Max because it spoiled the purity of the U, but it was barely visible from the ground.

Almost everybody loved the house, including the patio and the 125-by-35-foot garden. It was so popular in the art world that when we decided to move thirteen years later, scores of people protested and declared it a great loss to Chicago and to themselves personally. Some of the most prominent architects didn't like the house, but many others loved it. The Chicago chapter of the AIA awarded it best house of the year.

For us, it was a treasure, a fulfillment of our dreams, only tempered by the tragedy that Max didn't live to see its completion.

The ground-floor living room, with Anselm Kiefer's "Jerusalem," 1986, between doors leading to the courtyard

Top: Combined dining room and library, with custom-designed bookshelves made of tubular steel frames and ebonized walnut cabinetry

Bottom: Gordon's sketch for the bookshelves

Opposite: Entryway view looking west through the ground floor

The second-floor gallery had 950 square feet of viewing space and a large skylight overhead

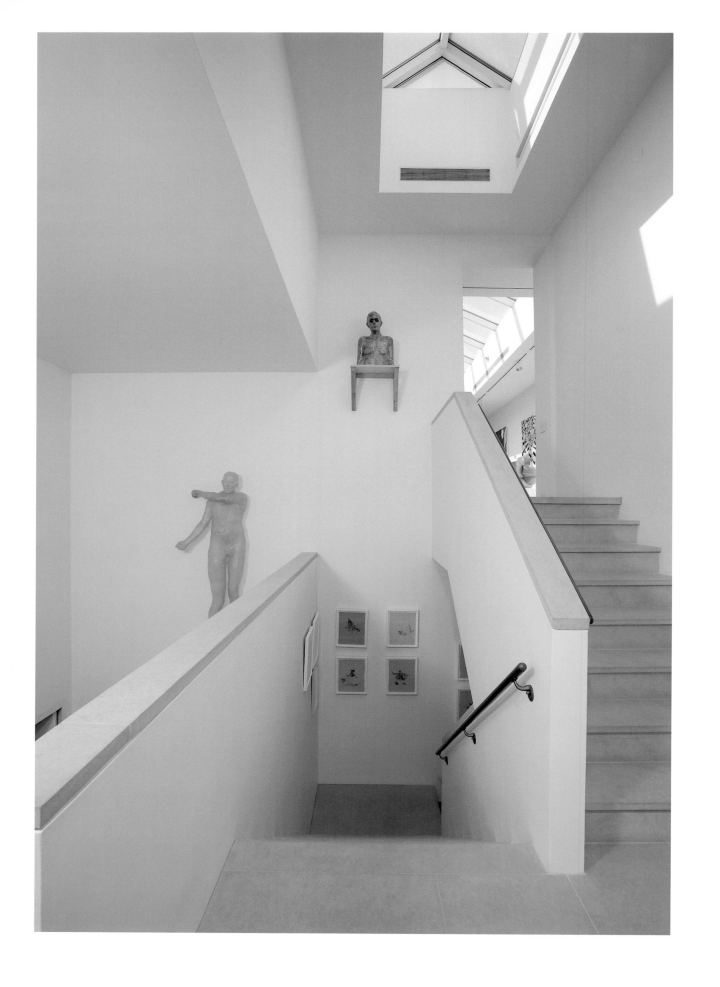

Left: A landing between the
first and second floors with
two Kiki Smith sculptures hung
top and left

Opposite: Views of the top
floor gallery, with an Eric Fischl
painting at right

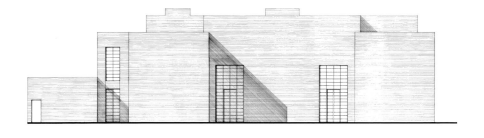

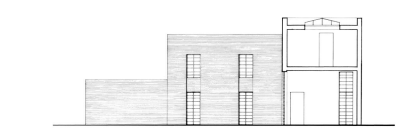

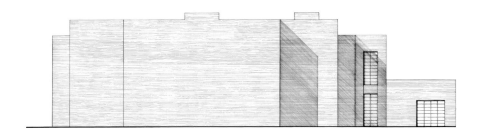

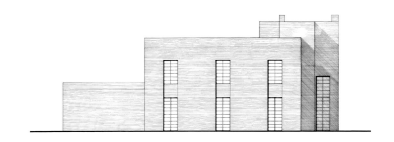

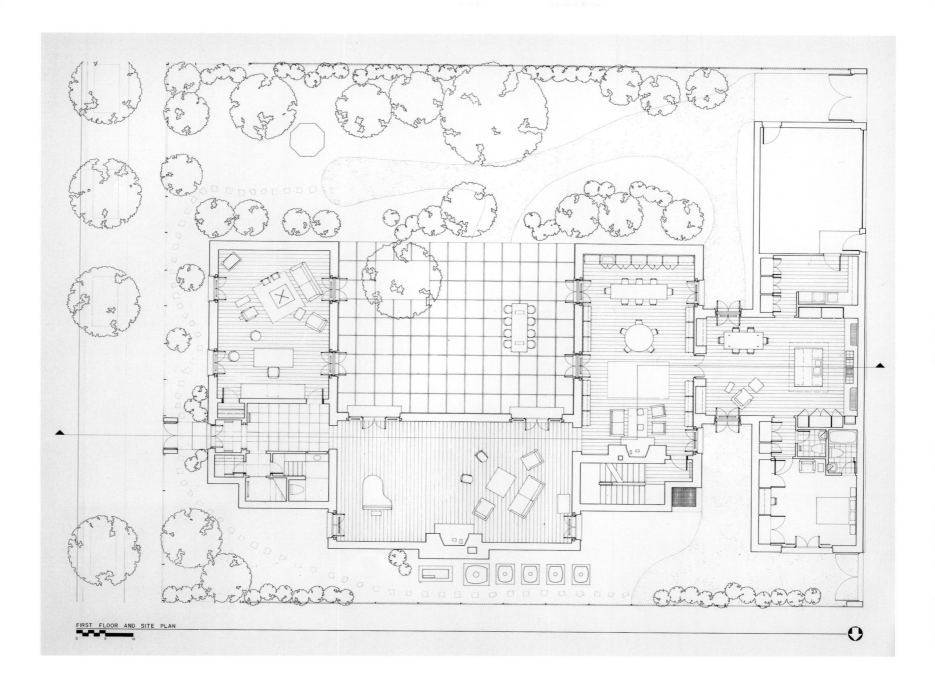

FIRST FLOOR AND SITE PLAN

Opposite, from top: South
elevation, east section, north
elevation, and east elevation

Above: First-floor plan and site
plan. The front door faces east.

The courtyard at dusk

The Fisher Landau Center for Art

Queens, New York, 1989–1992

Emily Fisher Landau

I had been collecting modern art and had some fine pieces by Picasso, Matisse, and Dubuffet, but I became interested in younger, living artists. My friend Bill Katz helped get me started and we began buying a lot of work. We could not get things into the apartment because the service elevator was too small, and everything I wanted to look at was in storage, so I decided to find a building. We found a 25,000-square-foot former parachute-harness factory in Queens. I then went on a tour of Europe to look at every private museum I could find. I was very thorough and went back to some of them twice. I went to the Boundary Road home of the Saatchi collection in London. I remember big spaces, and a caretaker's apartment by the entrance. It was the one I liked best by far. I told Bill, and he said he knew the architect, Max Gordon. He introduced us, and we went to see the building. Max got excited and said he would work with us.

It was such a delight. He would do sketches and wave his arms around and discuss concepts and then refine them and come back. It was like a seminar.

He was also so practical and economical. He said that in ten years I might change my mind and want to convert the building into lofts, so he insisted that each floor be self-contained, with its own air-conditioning and heating, bathrooms, and utility meters. He put in a whole floor of storage in the basement and, as at Boundary Road, an apartment for a custodian. He hid the windows with screens concealing built-in artificial lights so that we did not have to replace the old window frames. This created plenty of soft, diffused light day and night. The building was not a perfect rectangle, more of a trapezoid shape, so he squared it off with artificial walls behind which we could have storage, electrics, and other services. On the second floor he fitted in pull-out racks for small works with a screen on the front so that we could show videos. We were required to have a handicap ramp, but instead of an unsightly afterthought, he made a long and elegant processional entry accessible for everyone. He made a space for trucks to pull in and unload behind locked gates, which was good security.

Max died before the job was finished so Bill Katz, who had been going to meetings with Max, and instead of Max if he was out of town, took over. He did the library and the reception desks. Indeed Bill learned so much from Max that he now has a successful practice designing spaces in the way that Max pioneered, doing the basic concept and then getting an associate architect to do the working drawings and together supervising construction. He has just finished designing a *hôtel particulier* and a huge studio for Anselm Kiefer in Paris.

Max did an incredible job, absolutely brilliant. It has stood the test of time. Clarity. Calm. Nothing to displease the eye. I'm very proud.

Exterior view of the three-story building in Queens

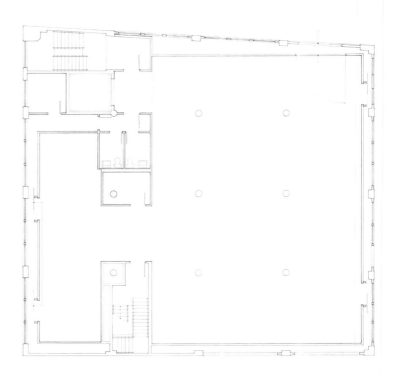

Above left: First-floor plan

Above right: Second-floor plan

Opposite: First-floor gallery, with Carl Andre's "Paraglyph," 1989, on the floor in the foreground, and Barbara Kruger's "Untitled (Pledge)," 1988, and "Heart," 1988 on the rear wall. Gordon had every gallery wall painted white, with poured concrete floors, polished and unsealed.

First-floor gallery with Gary
Hume's "The Outsider," 2005,
in the foreground. Robert
Rauschenberg's "Soviet/
American Array," 1988–90,
is on the rear wall.

Opposite: A gallery flooded
with natural light

Above: Gallery on the third floor

Above: Gordon's sliding storage system for the second floor showing Keith Haring's "Untitled," 1985

Opposite: An example of Gordon's Synskin lighting: synthetic fabric masks the windows and diffuses natural light, while fluorescent tubes provide a constant glow

Opposite, top: The reception
area with Jon Kessler's "City,"
1989, left, and Andy Warhol's
"Portrait of Emily Fisher Landau," 1984, right

Opposite, bottom: The library
was completed by Bill Katz.
Books are enclosed in tidy
matching containers.

Above: The main entrance at
the north side of the building is
also the accessibility ramp

Signature Characteristics

Jonathan Marvel

Max Gordon liked to create even, minimally shaped, quiet volumes which call attention to paintings and sculptures rather than to the architecture itself. He relied on a proportionate system of squares and double squares in his freestanding structures, like the U-shaped Manilow House, with its three-volume massing, or like the Sachs residence, with its perfect-square living room. He rigorously stuck to this proportional credo even when he was renovating an existing building, such as the three-story Fisher Landau Center for Art. For this project, Gordon used floating walls to create an approximate 1:1.6 Golden Ratio viewing gallery on each level, turning the existing mushroom columns into space-defining elements and reconfiguring them on each level to include four, then six, then finally eight exposed columns on the top floor.

Gordon was concerned with the way people circulated through a space: in a gallery, he wanted viewers to move through a sequence of rooms so as to optimize their experience of the art. Typically, Gordon would initiate the sequence of spaces with a foyer and conceal incidentals, such as reception desks or shelves, leaving the rest of the experience at the service of art. At Annely Juda Fine Art, he combined the front desk, meeting room, and shelving into a reception area, and cut a symmetrical opening in a thick wall through which the visitor crosses into the main gallery space. From the reception area of Boundary Road, the visitor dramatically descended stairs into the main exhibition area.

At 120 Mount Street, he experimented with the idea of eliminating hallways and ornament, as he did in his two previous apartments: the circular elevator wall was transformed to be the dominant element in the space, arranging the study, library, and living room around it. The classical notion of *enfilade*, where one space opens into the next, was used in all his projects, but it is represented best in the Manilow House where the three double-square volumes—study, living room, dining room—lead into one another through double-height doorways. In a letter about the Manilow House to an associate, Gordon wrote, "The massing of the building is rather eccentric; it looks like a mixture of the Wittgenstein House and a Mario Botta house." These references to interlocking unadorned spaces are consistent with Gordon's fondness for simple box-shaped volumes with single large openings, and for rooms that open into one another.

Lighting was a key design element for Gordon. He hated naked bulbs or tubes: at Boundary Road he put them in troughs to uplight the roof and diffuse light. He used the threshold between rooms to mark transitions as one moves through spatial sequence: the lighting sometimes begins as electric and concludes as natural light flooding a main space. The main gallery at Boundary Road; the gallery at Annely Juda, illuminated by its forty-foot-long skylight; the top-floor reading room at the Fisher Landau Center; and the double-height living room at the Manilow House all follow this pattern.

A complete lack of ornament was another signature. At the Brody Residence in New York, the fireplace mantels stood out as sculptural objects against the clean white walls stripped of baseboard and crown molding. At the stair, he revealed his playful side with an upside-down stepped light fixture based on the dentils from the molding. At Brody, as with nearly all his projects, his use of "Synskin light," a fiberglass scrim that filters daylight and fluorescent light, evenly illuminated the spaces at all hours.

Gordon's greatest architectural achievement was the ability to create a unified whole, spaces where the details do not attract too much attention, thus allowing the relationship between the viewer and the art, and not the viewer and the architecture, to be the primary experience.

Chronology

Chronology

Fig. 1: Greencoat Place

1931

June 10—Born Cape Town, South Africa.

1937

Gordon family moved to England.

1949–52

Attended Christ's College, Cambridge, graduated with an M.A. in architecture.

1952–55

Attended the Architectural Association, London, graduated with a Diploma.

1955–56

Attended Harvard Graduate School of Design, Cambridge, Mass., graduated with an M.Arch.

1956

Became an Associate of the Royal Institute of British Architects.

1956–62

Design architect at Skidmore, Owings & Merrill, New York, where he worked on the midtown branch of Chase Manhattan Bank, New York, and Banque Lambert, Brussels.
Roger Radford: "In those years I was the project designer, working under the direction of Gordon Bunshaft, on a variety of projects and Max was a very valuable part of my team. Bunshaft not only directed the design but was a very strong aesthetic influence. In particular he was an avid art collector and always tried to integrate art into his buildings, often with success, as with David Rockefeller at Chase: so much depended on the owners."

1962–68

Moved back to England, remodeled and lived in a small terrace house at 55, Greencoat Place, Victoria (fig. 1), his first of three London homes.

1962–70

Partner at Chapman, Taylor and Partners, London, where he designed: New Scotland Yard, 2-10 Broadway, London; Rank Hovis McDougall headquarters, London; Commercial Plastics (Unilever) factory, Cramlington; apartment for Sir Isaac

Wolfson on Portland Place, London (fig. 2); banking hall, Hill Samuel, St James's Square, London.

1968–76

Remodeled and lived in the first-floor apartment at 29, Belgrave Square, Belgravia (fig. 3).

1970–81

Partner at Louis de Soissons and Partners, Luton, Bedfordshire, and London, where his designs included: City Club, London; Gordon's own apartment, 120 Mount Street, London; house and pool for Rafael Navarro, Buckinghamshire.

1972

Joined the International Council of the Museum of Modern Art, New York, recommended by committee members Joanne Stern and Lily Auchincloss.

1972–77

Trustee of the Contemporary Art Society, an organization that buys contemporary art and donates it to art museums in Britain. In 1974 Gordon was one of the two art purchasers for the year. His selection was notably international and included the German artist Peter Kalkhof, Canadian-born artist Dorothea Rockburne, and four Americans: Brice Marden, Agnes Martin, Bruce Nauman, and Richard Serra.

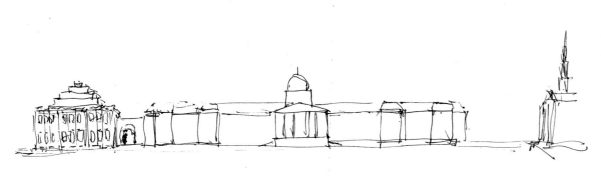

Fig. 4: Early concept drawing of the London National Gallery extension in the style of John Nash

1977–90

Remodeled and lived in the fourth-floor apartment at 120 Mount Street, Mayfair, an Edwardian building with one apartment per floor. The other residents, all prominent in the art world, all died prematurely of AIDS: Adrian Ward-Jackson, David Carritt, and Harry Bailey.

1978

Invited to be an advisor to the 1979 International Architecture Prize (later known as the Pritzker Prize) and submit nominations.

1980

Jasper Johns House
Saint Martin
Jasper Johns: "Max visited me in Saint Martin where I had a house I was hoping to alter or replace with a new one. I believe it was while he was there that he sketched ideas for what he thought might be interesting. He later sent me a little book of dreams about the Queen, who apparently frequently appears in the dreams of the English."

1981

Established Max Gordon Associates.

1980s

Marlborough Fine Art
Albemarle Street, London
Associate architect: Richard Goldsbrough
Gordon worked on various remodelings of the gallery and offices throughout the 1980s. He also designed a graphics gallery for Marlborough on Dover Street.

1982

The National Gallery Extension (fig. 4)
London
A competition was held for an extension to the National Gallery. Gordon created a design in the style of architect John Nash.

Saatchi and Saatchi Head Office
Charlotte Street, London
Consulted on use of space.

1982–83

Jennifer Bartlett Apartment
21 rue Vavin, Paris
Gordon cleared away a rabbit warren of small rooms to create large spaces including a studio in this elegant art deco building in Montparnasse.

1982–88

The Economist Newspaper Ltd
London
Max acted as a consultant to The Economist Group—where his brother David was CEO—on architectural matters for The Economist Building and for The Economist Intelligence Unit. The Economist Building, designed by Peter and Alison Smithson, opened in 1964 and needed renovation. Max recommended Skidmore, Owings & Merrill, and they were appointed in 1986.

1983–84

Seligman Apartment

Park Street, London

Associate architect: Richard Goldsbrough
Gordon met Goldsbrough on this job through interior designers Tessa Kennedy and Finola Sumner. He went on to become Gordon's associate architect in England.

1983–85

98a Boundary Road (Saatchi Gallery)

London

1985

Brooke Alexander Gallery (fig. 5)

59 Wooster Street, New York City

Associate architect: Richard Gluckman
Brooke Alexander: "We had two or three all-night sessions where Max would draw various schematics of the floor plan on that flimsy tracing paper. We worked out one that I liked, but it was not at all what he wanted. He said, "Okay, that's one. Now try this!" And he created essentially this one big space. The windows were covered by a wall. The idea was that you go up the stairs or you get off the elevator and enter into a kind of city square. Everything else, as far as he was concerned, was secondary. Max could be quite persuasive."

Elizabeth Murray and Bob Holman Apartment

17 White Street, New York City (fig. 6)

Associate architect: Richard Gluckman
Bob Holman: "Elizabeth and I got to know Max in the early 1970s. In those days, the gang that was hanging out around the Paula Cooper Gallery was a kind of sprawling commune. Even though they were each such individualists in their art, it seemed like nobody could have a doctor, an astrologer, a shrink or an architect without everybody agreeing that this was the best possible choice. And once that was made, everybody joined in.

And the official architect was Max. That's one I could understand. He was an artist just like everybody else. When he went to work it was right in your

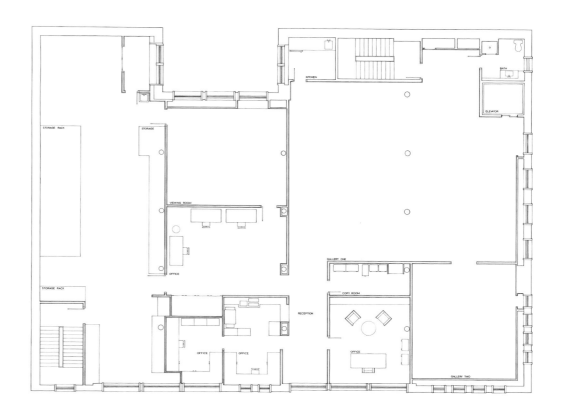

Fig. 5: Floor plan, Brooke Alexander Gallery

Fig. 6: Floor plan for Murray–Holman apartment

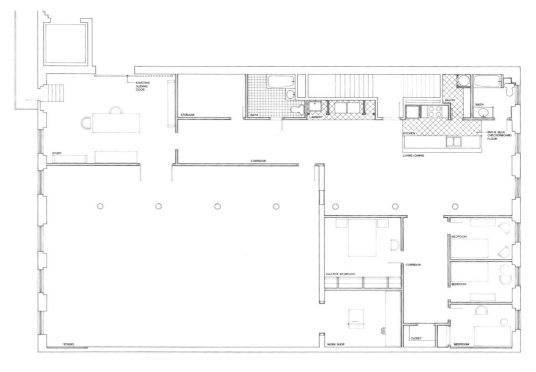

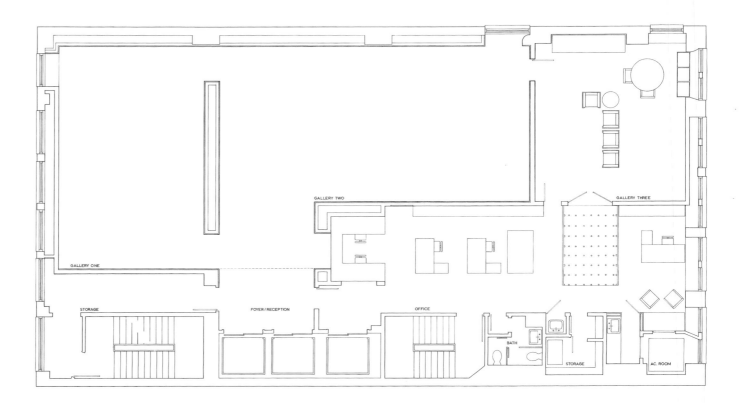

Fig. 7: Galerie Maeght Lelong
floor plan

flat, right in your loft. And his shirtsleeves would get rolled up, his cigarette would dangle from his mouth, and he would get this expression where you could tell that he was taking everything in, but it was almost catatonic. His eyes seemed to glaze over as he made sketches with his hands in the air. He would wander; he would pace looking at this space and that space and really was in another world. You'd be standing there beside him; one minute you're in conversation and the next he's inside the geometries of the space as if he were part of it. He was completely obsessed with whatever it was that he was doing, even if it was, in this case, something as mundane as changing our crazy "homemade loft" into something that would have the look and feel of a finished classic: a simple space with bedrooms for our two new daughters who were, at that point, two and a newborn, and our son, who was in high school. And my office, a poet's garret, and Elizabeth's magnificent studio space, which we would, after we left, miss forever. We were there for seven or eight years.

He created a kind of island for the kitchen that became known as the "Daisy 500," after the Indianapolis 500, so called because Daisy, who was just born at this time, as she grew up, took this island to be her own private race course. Behind it Max put in big linoleumlike red and blue tiles that really popped. While the loft was classic Soho—steel columns and straight-edge walls, lots of light from the windows—behind the counters and the island was this moment of sheer exuberance. It was very reminiscent of the kinds of colors that Elizabeth used. The girls each had their bedroom: Dakota's room had been a kind of quarter circle, it had an arc along it. Max jimmied that into a regularity that really made it feel much calmer with a classic feel to it, although it was nothing but modern. Our room was the only one that didn't change."

1985–86

Galerie Maeght Lelong (fig. 7)
57th Street, New York City
Associate architect: Richard Gluckman
Maeght Lelong and Brooke Alexander were the first galleries on which Gordon and Richard Gluckman collaborated. Richard Gluckman: "Max understood how a gallery worked—the flow of people into a gallery, the progression of space, the movement into the showroom, the relationship of the workings of the gallery, the need for storage.

All of this was far more important than just the main exhibition space. That is why he was trusted by dealers. In everything that he did, almost every decision that he made in the design of the gallery, he was not trying to be a minimalist, but to minimize the impact of architecture and design on the experience of viewing the art.

He had his tricks. We were once in a meeting with a contractor and he starts speaking in a way that was unintelligible. And I said afterwards, "Max, I didn't quite understand that," and he said, "Of course. I didn't have an answer so when I don't have an answer, I try to make myself as incoherent as possible and since I have a British accent, they think I know what I'm talking about."

The association with Gluckman lasted for four years. During this period Gluckman also worked on galleries independently of Gordon. In 1988 Gordon was encouraged to enter the competition to design MASS MoCA and expected to work with Gluckman, only to discover that Gluckman had entered the competition with a different group. Max thereafter worked with other architects as associates.

Fig. 8: Dagny Corcoran apartment

Fig. 9: Bryan and Lucy Ferry apartment

Dagny Corcoran Apartment (fig. 8)
London
Associate architect: Richard Goldsbrough

Charles Cowles Apartment
27 West 67th Street, New York City
Associate architect: Richard Gluckman
Richard Gluckman: "This job and Koury Wingate are where he used Synskin [translucent light-diffusing material made of glass fiber supplied in rolls] to the best effect. In Charlie's, the scale of the Synskin on large double-height windows in a north-facing room was terrific. The Synskin windows were a great contribution: to put artificial light at the source of where natural light came from so that the function of the window during the evening would be the same as during the day."

1985–87

Bryan and Lucy Ferry Apartment (fig. 9)
New York City
Associate Architect: Richard Gluckman

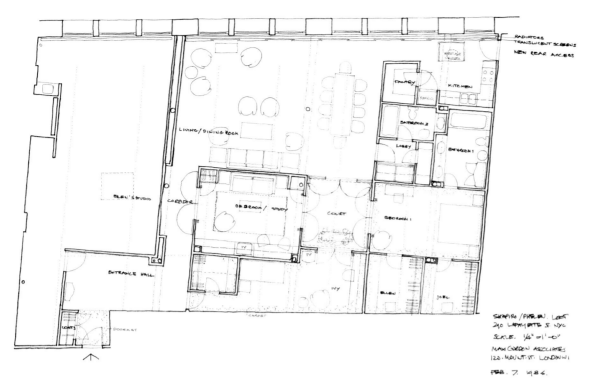

Fig. 10: Phelan–Shapiro loft

James Corcoran Gallery Santa Monica
Los Angeles, California
Associate architect: Sue O'Brien
Max took his fee in the form of stays at the Pritikin health spa.

Ellen Phelan and Joel Shapiro Loft (fig. 10)
Lafayette Street, New York City
Associate architect: Richard Gluckman

1985–89

John Kaldor Fabric Showroom
4 Great Portland Street, London
Associate architect: Richard Goldsbrough

1985–90

Anthony d'Offay Gallery
London
Associate architect: Richard Goldsbrough
The gallery occupied various spaces on Dering Street.

1986

Robert J. Pierot Apartment
Park Avenue, New York City

Robert and Sally Benton Apartment
1065 Lexington Avenue, New York City

1986–90

Museo Nacional Centro de Arte Reina Sofía
Madrid
The Reina Sofía building was designed by Francesco Sabatini (1722–97) as the Hospital de San Carlos. The Spanish government appointed Carmen Gimenez, an independent curator, well-known for *Correspondencias*, an important exhibition in 1982 on sculpture and architecture, as special adviser to the ministry of culture in 1983. Her brief was to put Spain and Spanish artists on the international map for modern and contemporary art. In 1984 she was appointed director of the National Center for Exhibitions for the Spanish Ministry of Culture and began convincing the Minister of Culture, Javier Solana, of the importance of keeping the hospital as a space solely dedicated to art. In 1986 Gimenez directed the opening exhibition using large spaces on the first and second floors of the Sabatini building, which was then renamed Museo Nacional Centro de Arte Reina Sofía.

She turned to Gordon for advice and he helped her get as far as possible back to the Sabatini. He also advised on the installation of exhibitions between 1986 and 1988. In an early report to Gimenez Gordon wrote: "The architecture space of the galleries is very beautiful and powerful already, and it is therefore necessary to minimize the impact of the details. . . . It is important that the floor surface is unobtrusive; as marble is already being installed, this should not be shiny, nor should there be any patterns in the laying of the floor slabs. Veins in the marble should be kept to a minimum. . . . Many of the hose reels and electrical switch boxes are still in positions that are too prominent."

Gimenez was also appointed to an architectural commission to advise on the whole building. The

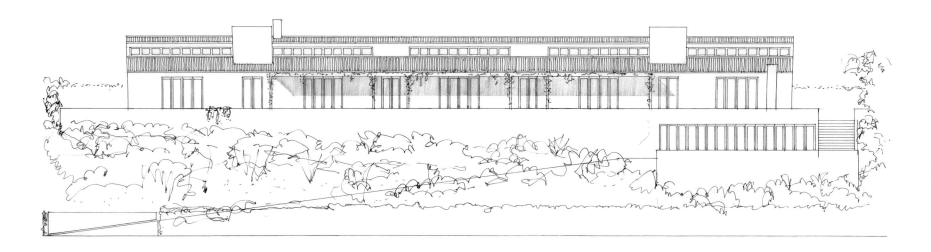

Fig. 11: Elevation of the unbuilt
Martin–Tennant house

government felt the building was large enough
to house other museums and a performing art
space. Gimenez fought against this. In 1987 she
invited Gordon, Nicholas Serota (then director of
the Whitechapel before going to the Tate), and Edy
de Wilde, who had just retired as director of the
Rijksmuseum Stedelijk in Amsterdam, on to the
commission. In 1988 a director was appointed to
the Reina Sofía and a year later Gimenez resigned.
The battle for simplicity and clarity was lost and
the spaces became over-designed. A letter from
Gordon to the ministry dated January 1989 criticized a series of interventions: "Now that the plaza
is being restored, it is clear that it is going to be
very handsome and it seems very perverse that the
only good façade that the Reina Sofía has will be
spoilt [by elevators]."

Subsequently Gimenez opened the Museo Picasso
in Málaga in 2003.

Carmen Gimenez: "Max came to Madrid in February
1986. We were due to open in May. There were
many things that he did not like that would have
been impossible to change in the time, and so he
concentrated on the essentials. I learned so much
from him: the moment you touch too much, you
destroy. Preserve the beauty that is there. Use
natural light if possible: don't close up windows
because daylight is better. Later, when I was working on the Museo Picasso (with Richard Gluckman)
I kept asking myself 'What would Max do?' Rather
than knock down the dilapidated houses in what
was then a rather junky neighborhood I decided to

incorporate them—destroy as little as possible.
We kept the spirit of the place—and that was
Max's influence.

Max was a special person in my life. I really loved
him very much. He was both an architect and an
artist, very much like a sculptor: he had a sense of
space and practicality. I don't think he wanted to
be a big architect. He wanted to be just the special
person he was, happy with people who understood him. He encouraged me to fight to keep the
character of a place, but to know when to accept
the reality set by the mediocrities; he himself was
not a fighter. He wanted to give me the energy to
fight for simplicity, for clean space, for light, against
stupidity; and my life has been spent fighting."

1987

House for Steve Martin and
Victoria Tennant (fig. 11)
Beverly Hills, California
This was never built because the clients decided to
buy an apartment in New York instead of building a
house in Los Angeles.

Jennifer Bartlett Apartment, 4th and 5th floors
237 Lafayette Street, New York City
Associate architect: Richard Gluckman
Jennifer Bartlett: "Working with Max was a real
give and take. There was detailing that was just
great—that little not-a-quarter-of-an-inch reveal at
the bottom of a wall. Very Max."

Fig. 12: Installation view of a Laurie Parsons show at the Lorence–Monk Gallery, May 1990. The show was the gallery, empty.

gallery in the East Village closed. Ealan Wingate: "The space was quite large compared to what we had before and we were concerned that the art would lose its sense of proportion and he got it spot on."

Cooper–Macrae House
West 21st Street, New York City
Remodeling of a house for Paula Cooper and Jack Macrae. It included an apartment where Gordon would stay in New York. Previously he stayed in an apartment at Paula Cooper's Wooster Street gallery.

San Francisco Museum of Modern Art
The Museum asked Gordon and some twenty other architects to submit portfolios for the competition to design the new SFMOMA. He was one of the final candidates. According to Jack Lane, then director: "I recall a lot of respect for Max's work, but what we knew were mostly his exemplary gallery spaces rather than large, up-from-the-ground buildings."

Ed Marschner Residence
96 Prince Street, New York City
Associate architect: Richard Gluckman

1987–88

Mayfair Fine Art
40–41 Conduit Street, London
Associate architect: Richard Goldsbrough

Asher Edelman Apartment
120 East End Avenue, New York City
Associate architect: Richard Gluckman

1987–90

Eugene and Jackie Brody House
119 East 79th Street, New York City
Associate architect: Richard Gluckman

1988

Koury Wingate Gallery
578 Broadway, New York City
Associate architect: Richard Gluckman
Ealan Wingate opened a Soho gallery with Elizabeth Koury after the International with Monument

1988–89

Richard and Clara Serra Loft
New York City
Associate architect: Richard Gluckman
Richard Serra: "When he first came he said, 'Just show me how you live.' And we said, 'Okay, there's a main wall down the middle and there's a kitchen in the back and then you walk around to an office and that follows around to a bedroom. So basically, the wall down the center divides the space in two elongated rectangles where you have continuous circulation.' And he said, 'Oh, that's fine, we're just going to keep it that way. We're not going to change a thing. We're just going to give you a vestibule. We're not going to have open entryways, we're going to have real doors and real rooms.' And he put it back together in a way that kept the floor plan the way it was, but provided for amenities that we didn't have and just for bigger volumes and more comforting situations and we took it in our stride and thought, 'Great!'"

Lorence–Monk Gallery (fig. 12)
568/578 Broadway, New York City
Associate architect: Andrew Ong

Susan Lorence: "We were initially at 568 Broadway and we took a new space right across the hall, about 3,000 square feet. Bob [Monk] and I were on a trip and on the plane we sketched what we wanted the gallery to look like on a napkin. When we got back I called Max because he was the only architect I knew of that would not want to impose his vision on our vision, and who would take what we wanted and make it into a reality without fussing it up.

I remember he came, looked around, and signed his name on the napkin and that was it. The space was on the top floor and had two skylights and windows that looked west clear above the other buildings and so the light was very, very beautiful both in the back of the space and in the front, with great views over Soho and lower Manhattan. We were very strict about having the fewest number of electrical outlets so that there were the least number of interruptions in the walls. Most of the artists were very minimal, so we were adamant about not having graphic elements, like electrical outlets, near where we were hanging pictures."

Bob Monk: "The gallery really was the perfect blank space. Even the columns that ran down the middle seemed to disappear because he was such a master of proportion. He boxed in the front windows with those [Synskin] shades that diffused the light beautifully.

We were there from 1988 to 1992. We left because the economy was bad and because the old hydraulic elevators could not cope with the increased traffic in a building in transition from one sweatshop per floor to multiple tenants.

The best photograph would probably be a shot of a show by Laurie Parsons in 1990. The show was simply the gallery, empty. I'm sure Max had as much of an ego as anybody else, but he was completely in tune with that time of the minimal aesthetic for visual arts, a time of a certain restraint and idealism, so the Laurie Parsons idea of the empty gallery—and of course the way that Max would design a gallery—will become not only a legacy of Max,

Fig. 13: Installation view of a group show, with a Cady Noland work pictured, at Luhring Augustine, 1991

but of the resurgence of interest in a particular time in the history of contemporary art."

Sutton Place Foundation for Fine Art: Storage
Surrey, England
Associate architect: Richard Goldsbrough
Plans were drawn up for a stand-alone art storage building, but it was not built once owner Fred Koch decided to sell the property.

Irwin Joffe House
6 Westmoreland Place, London
Associate architect: Richard Goldsbrough
Remodeling of a terrace house.

Luhring Augustine Gallery (fig. 13)
130 Prince Street, New York City
Associate architect: Richard Gluckman and David Acheson

Lawrence Luhring: "My partner, Roland Augustine, and I admired a couple of spaces that Max had designed. In 1989 we decided to buy out our third partner and move to Soho, which made more sense for what we were doing. We both admired Paula Cooper's gallery in Soho and also the Saatchi

127

Collection [Boundary Road] in London and Max came to mind as someone that we both admired and would do a terrific job. We did not know him. I think Paula made the introduction.

Roland and I met Max at the space and then went for lunch. We sat and just talked about art and what we liked about the spaces that Max had done; it was a very relaxed conversation. We were a young gallery, not very known, and Max was a very well-known architect and I just remember he treated us with a great deal of respect and listened intently. He made a drawing on a napkin of the basic design—and that in essence became the gallery. Richard Gluckman did the working drawings and then David Acheson supervised the construction.

I remember going and looking at lighting with Max—we chose Lightolier, very basic, raw bulbs. We were working with a tight budget. But at the time, this was completely adequate and was standard in a Soho gallery.

We spent a lot of time with Max talking about how the aperture for the reception should be and it's been hard to replicate in our other galleries. One always has this problem with people putting their elbows on the shelf and looking in at what the receptionist is doing, what mail is there, what transparencies are on the desk. So we worked on the size and height of that opening so that it wasn't comfortable to lean on and look in, yet large enough so that the receptionist had a full view of the gallery and of the proceedings going on.

The contractor poured a beautiful concrete floor. He had a kid come in and clean the floor with acid. It ate the finish off the floor and left wipe marks. I was distraught. We went to the contractor and he didn't see the problem. He assumed the concrete floor would be covered. But Max said, 'It's fine. It looks like an old floor.' And artists loved it! But it was really hard for me and Max's encouragement was important.

We opened in January 1990. Sadly we lost most of our photos and papers in a flood here. Subsequently we opened a gallery in L.A., another uptown in New York on Madison Avenue, and now this space here in Chelsea, but Roland and I both feel that space in Soho was, by far, our favorite.

Roland and I had a small office behind the reception area and Bill Katz, the artist who became an architect, thought it was the most beautiful space in New York. He used to bring people in all the time and say, 'May I show your office?' It was a beautifully proportioned room, just incredible. It had a natural feel.

For us, being new gallerists, it gave us a lot of confidence to work with Max. He gave us a beautiful space at a time people knew the Saatchi space; and there was a certain cachet to having a serious architect like Max take us seriously enough to work with us."

1988–90

P.S. 1 Contemporary Art Center
Long Island City, Queens
Director Alanna Heiss showed Gordon the plans drawn up by the architect who had already been appointed. Max criticized them severely. Alanna Heiss: "He looked and said, 'Well, you can't have this.' It was just definitive. 'You have to get another architect.' I stewed for a couple of months and found out that the contract with the architect could not be broken.

I had another meeting with Max. Same thing, 'You can't let this happen! This is your responsibility, you're the person in charge.' He was outraged. But he also did not have the time to get involved. So I tried to think of a way that I could have Max's ideas and his reputation. Max had a tremendous reputation at this point. He had done the Saatchi Gallery. He had done Scotland Yard.

So I concocted this scheme: an architecture committee. I used his name to get two other architects, but I didn't tell them that Max hadn't agreed to be on the committee yet. I went to Richard Gluckman. I went to Fred Fisher, from the West Coast, a real gentleman. I told the Board that we had an architectural review committee of three, headed by Max Gordon, that was going to review the plans and decide what we were going to do. Max became more elusive as he tried to separate himself from a looming disaster. When I got hold of him, I threatened to tell everybody that I had gone to him for advice and he had abandoned me. So he accepted to join the committee.

We didn't have money to fly members of the committee in so we met in hotel lobbies when Max was in town on some other job. So we're seated in this lobby of this hotel: Max was in the center flanked by the west coast and the east coast and I was the other side, I was the south pole. I put the model of P.S. 1 down on the table and Max said, 'As you can see, this will never do.' So then we started about architecture and art. It was a wonderful experience. Everyone had their own ideas, but the problem was how to get any of them implemented. In the end the board and the city got the architect to accept Fred Fisher as a consultant.

This was not just Max being an architect, but Max being a friend to art and a friend to me, whom he didn't know very well. He really knew how to curate art; he hung it perfectly, he had perfect pitch. These are areas of specialization that caused me to see Max as a god."

Fig. 14: Andy Warhol exhibition at the Hayward Gallery

1988–96

Paul J. Schupf Wing for the Works of Alex Katz
Colby College Museum of Art
Waterville, Maine
Completion architect: Scott Teas of TFH Architects
Alex Katz, the artist, Gordon's friend since the 1970s, was an admirer of the Boundary Road gallery. Conceptual drawings were discussed with Alex Katz and the university in 1988, but Gordon had died by the time funds had been raised. The building, completed by Scott Teas, expanded on Gordon's scheme but respected his design.

1989

Dakis Joannou House and Gallery
Athens
These projects were never completed.

Solomon R. Guggenheim Museum
New York City
Consultancy.

Anthony and Anne d'Offay Residence
7 Chester Terrace, London
Associate architect: Richard Goldsbrough

Andy Warhol Exhibition (fig. 14)
Hayward Gallery, London
Gordon was the designer for this art exhibition held at the Hayward Gallery, part of the Southbank Centre. The building is unwelcoming concrete. Max covered up the parts he found uncongenial with white scrim.

Salama Caro Gallery
5–6 Cork Street, London
Associate architect: Richard Goldsbrough

Marlborough Fine Art
Merton Road, London
Associate architect: Richard Goldsbrough
Conversion of an industrial warehouse into an out-of-town storage area with a large open space to show sculpture to clients.

Fig. 15: Per Kirkeby retrospective, Galerie Forsblom, Helsinki, 1990

Saatchi & Saatchi Head Office
Berkeley Square, London
Consultant on space utilization.

1989–90

Waddington Galleries
12 Cork Street, London
Associate architect: Richard Goldsbrough

Leslie and Clodagh Waddington Apartment
8 Cheyne Gardens, London
Associate architect: Richard Goldsbrough

Galerie Forsblom (fig. 15)
Helsinki
Associate architect: Jaako Antti-Poika of Terasto
Kaj Forsblom: "I had a gallery in Helsinki already but decided to open another space. I saw the Saatchi Collection in London and loved the architecture, the simplicity of his design, and how Max respected the works of art. I knew of Max but did not know him. I invited him to Helsinki for one summer weekend in 1989.

Since we needed a Finnish architect I asked an up-and-coming young architect to join us at the space, 11, Yrjönkatu, an early 1900s building with a courtyard. But he misunderstood the idea. He thought he would be doing the design himself rather than just doing the working drawings. It became an awkward situation but Max said, 'Give me two hours and I can make a sketch.' The young architect started to laugh and said, 'You can't do anything in two hours.' Max went to the hotel and we met up in two, two and a half hours, and Max had a clear sketch of the whole gallery. And then this young architect became completely silent. He didn't say a word and he left and I have never seen him since.

I invited Jaako Antti-Poika of Terasto to be the associate architect. He later became the restoration architect for the island fortress called Suomenlinna. We started at the end of August and finished in the spring of 1990. Max found a way to make the floor very strong in order to support stone and steel sculptures. Apart from the details for the offices and such, everything was exactly according to the original sketch. No difference whatsoever. The result was a very simple space—Max had the talent to see how to make it simple."

Sylvia Simon Studio
70 Grand Street, New York City
Associate architect: Andrew Ong

Richard L. Feigen Gallery
London
This project for a London branch of the New York gallery did not go ahead.

Dennis Holtz Fine Art
9 Cork Street, London
Associate architect: Richard Goldsbrough

Annely Juda Fine Art
23 Dering Street, London
Associate architect: Richard Goldsbrough

Addition to Sachs House
Philadelphia, Pennsylvania
Associate architect: The Klett Organization

1989–92

Manilow House
North Howe Street, Chicago
Associate architect: John Vinci of Vinci Hamp
Architects
The Manilows moved out in 2008. The new owners
retained John Vinci to add a wing that closed off
the U-shape.

Fisher Landau Center for Art
38–27 30th Street, Long Island City, Queens
Associate architect: David Acheson, Acheson Doyle
Partners

1990

Studio for Anselm Kiefer
Buchen
Not completed.

Museum for Contemporary Art Stuttgart
Stuttgart
Asked to join the competition.

Instituto Valenciano de Arte Moderno (IVAM)
Valencia
Study of exhibition lighting.

August 23—Died, London, England.

1992

No Trim: the Architecture of Max Gordon exhibition at the Architecture Foundation, London,
April 28–May 29. Director of the Architecture
Foundation: Richard Burdett. Curator of the
exhibition: Doris Lockhart Saatchi.

Howard Hodgkin, "Memories
of Max," 1991–95

Illustration credits

Imprint

Picture credits are listed by page number. Illustrations are by Max Gordon unless otherwise identified. Every effort was made to identify sources, but the publisher will endeavor to rectify any inadvertent omissions.

t=top, b=bottom

Courtesy Annely Juda Fine Art, London: **70–74, 77**
© 2010 Artists Rights Society (ARS), New York/ADAGP, Paris/F.L.C.: **14(b)**
Richard Bryant © The World of Interiors, March 1987: **53**
© 2004 Waye Cable: **93–96, 100–101**
Chapman Taylor Partners: **24**
Chicago History Museum/Bill Engdahl: **26**
D. James Dee, Courtesy of the artist & Matthew Marks Gallery: **22**
© Todd Eberle: **108**
Hermann Feldhaus: **106–7, 112(t)**
Fisher Landau Center for Art: **102, 105, 109–11, 112(b), 113**
Courtesy Galerie Forsblom, Helsinki: **130**
© 2010 Halkin Architectural Photography LLC: **78, 81–83, 85–87**
John M. Hall Photographs: **56, 59–67, 92(t), 97**
Courtesy Howard Hodgkin and Keith and Kathy Sachs: **133**
Ken Kirkwood © The World of Interiors, September 1982: **30, 37**
Rafael S. Lobato: **18**
Doris Lockhart Saatchi: **44–45, 51**
Courtesy of the artist and Luhring Augustine, New York: **127**
Jonathan Marvel/Rogers Marvel Architects: **104, 121–22**
Derry Moore: **35–36, 39**
Anthony Oliver: **52**
Courtesy Paula Cooper Gallery, New York: **21**
Gregory Phillips: **68**
© Yoshihiko Ueda: **10**
Vinci Hamp Architects: **98–99**
Fritz von der Shulenburg © The World of Interiors, 1987: **123(t)**
Photographer: Nicholas Walster. Courtesy of the Lorence-Monk Gallery
        records, 1961–1992, Archives of American Art, Smithsonian Institution: **126**

Copyright © 2010 David Gordon
All rights reserved. No part of this publication may be reproduced or transmitted in any form or by any means, electronic or mechanical, including photocopy, recording, or any information storage or retrieval system, without permission in writing from the publisher.

Cataloging-in-Publication Data is on file with the Library of Congress.

ISBN: 978–0–615–39579–1

This book is available through
D.A.P./Distributed Art Publishers, Inc.
155 6th Avenue, 2nd Floor
New York, NY 10013
Tel: (212) 627-1999
Fax: (212) 627-9484

Produced by Marquand Books, Inc., Seattle
www.marquand.com

Edited by Holly LaDue
Designed by Matthew Egan
Proofread by Maggi Gordon
Color Management by iocolor, Seattle
Printed and bound in China by
Artron Color Printing Co., Ltd.